Alternatives to Litigation

Alternatives to Litigation
Mediation, Arbitration, and
the Art of Dispute Resolution

Second Edition

Abraham P. Ordover and Andrea Doneff

National Institute for Trial Advocacy

NITA Editorial Board

Reproduction Permission
National Institute for Trial Advocacy
Notre Dame Law School
Notre Dame, Indiana 46556
(800) 225-6482   Fax (574) 271-8375
E-mail: nita.1@nd.edu   www.nita.org

Ordover, Abraham P., and Andrea Doneff, *Alternatives to Litigation: Mediation, Arbitration, and the Art of Dispute Resolution*, NITA, 2002.

Library of Congress Cataloging-in-Publication Data

Ordover, Abraham P., 1937-
    Alternatives to litigation : mediation, arbitration, and the art of dispute resolution / Abraham P. Ordover and Andrea Doneff.--2nd ed.
    p. cm.
    Includes bibliographical references and index.
    ISBN 1-55681-749-5
    1. Dispute resolution (Law)--United States. 2. Arbitration and award--United States. I. Doneff, Andrea, 1962- II. National Institute for Trial Advocacy (U.S.) III. Title.

KF9048 .O73 2002
347.73'9--dc21   2002073417

Second edition

Contents

Acknowledgments

The authors would like to thank the following people for their help in creating this book:

Kit Devine, for all her research assistance.

Pat Siuta, for her contribution of the chapter on Divorce Mediation.

Dan Klein, for his contribution of the materials on Decision Tree Analysis.

Dr. Beverly Schaffer, for her materials and ideas.

Raye Rawls, for the same.

Robbie Dokson, for his insight and help on the chapters on arbitration.

From Andrea—thank you to my family for supporting me through the writing of this book.

About the Authors

Abraham P. Ordover is president and CEO of Resolution Resources Corporation (RRC). He serves as an arbitrator, mediator, and neutral evaluator. Mr. Ordover mediates a wide variety of cases, and also has extensive experience as a commercial litigator. His specialty is mediating complex, often multiparty business disputes, including contract issues, corporate dissolutions, employment and environmental issues, personal injury matters, and professional malpractice and product liability issues.

A graduate of Syracuse University and Yale Law School, Mr. Ordover has taught evidence, trial practice, and civil procedure at Emory University and Hofstra, and trial practice and litigation techniques for the National Institute for Trial Advocacy (NITA).

Mr. Ordover has received teaching awards from the American College of Trial Lawyers and the Roscoe Pound American Trial Lawyer's Foundation. He has successfully mediated over a thousand cases and is a fellow of the American Academy of Civil Trial Mediators.

Andrea Doneff is one of the original principals of RRC and is vice president of the company. She is an experienced mediator and arbitrator, concentrating on business litigation that includes contracts, real estate, construction, and employment matters. Before joining RRC in 1991, Ms. Doneff clerked for Judge Marvin Shoob, now senior judge for the Northern District of Georgia, and practiced law with a major Atlanta law firm.

A graduate of Emory University and Emory University School of Law, Ms. Doneff is an adjunct professor at Emory University School of Law, where she teaches an upper-level course on ADR. Ms. Doneff also works with RRC's training group, teaching both public and private courses on negotiation, communication, mediation, and arbitration, among other topics.

CHAPTER ONE:
INTERESTS, RIGHTS, AND POWER

OVERVIEW

There are no limits on the causes of conflict. They may be economic, political, ethnic, national, or gender based. They may be the result of misbehavior, mistake, differences in concepts of right and wrong, differing value systems, misinformation, lack of information, poor communication, different concepts of what is relevant or important, or they may be based on the relations of the parties.

Whatever the causes, people and institutions find ways of resolving their conflicts. Some find a form of resolution in doing nothing. That is, they seek to avoid conflict by refusing to engage in it. This may take the form of actually denying that the problem exists. More likely, a decision will be made that the costs of resolving the disagreement may be greater than the effort to achieve success justifies. These costs (transaction costs) will be economic but also will have social and psychological components. The costs of dispute resolution include emotional and time investments, the impact on those affected by the ongoing dispute, and, if the dispute reaches the stage of litigation, legal expenses. All conflict resolution devices have transaction costs.

MEANS OF DISPUTE RESOLUTION

Most often, our society focuses on three means of dispute resolution. These are (1) rights-based, (2) power-based, and (3) interest-based. Our legal system is based on the premise that we have certain rights to be protected by laws and defended in a courtroom. Thus, when Party A believes that Party B has breached its contract, Party A will retain counsel and file a lawsuit to vindicate its rights. Adjudication, then, is one frequently followed path. In this mode one party will eventually emerge as the winner, its rights upheld and announced by a court of competent jurisdiction, while the other party loses the conflict.

A second widely used form of conflict resolution is based on the wielding of power by one party against another. The weapon of power may be political or economic. It may also be used in tandem with a rights-based or adjudicatory approach. Examples of the use of power to resolve disputes abound. These include the use by an employer of the power of the purse against a disfavored employee. The "boss" simply cuts the salary or refuses an increase or, worse, discharges the person. Any number of variations can be played on that theme. Employees can also use power. A union can use power against the employer, indeed against a whole industry, by calling a strike of the workers. The resulting paralysis may bring about the resolution that the union desires.

Power is often used in tandem with a rights adjudication. The party possessing the greater share of economic power over its rival will use that power to defeat its adversary in litigation. Money will be spent on discovery, motion practice, expert witnesses, and the like in a battle of attrition aimed at the collapse of the weaker combatant. If the transaction costs become too great to bear, the party least able to bear them may withdraw or accept a settlement far below what the case was thought to be worth. Worse, if the basis of the litigation is the definition of a right—a contract provision, a constitutional right, etc.—withdrawal by the economically weaker party may have consequences for many others who are not immediate parties to the action. Observation teaches us that if one has the power, he will use it to achieve his ends in conflict resolution as in all other endeavors.

In response to increasing dissatisfaction with solving conflicts through power or rights adjudications, both of which usually end up in a WIN-LOSE posture, there is a growing emphasis on interest-based resolution. In this approach to ending conflict, the parties seek to break the impasse through negotiation, often with the help of a mediator or other disinterested third party. Interest-based resolution does not focus on which party is "right." All too often both parties are "right" depending upon how you ask the question. Nor is the exercise of power decisive in getting past the dispute. Instead, through discussions the parties try to understand the nature of the problem they face, their individual interests to be protected, and the options available to solve the problem. The solution will seek to accommodate the interests of both parties in solving the problem. Where successful, the dispute will resolve in a WIN-WIN fashion.

We have defined rights and power. Interests are easy enough to articulate generally but sometimes difficult to uncover in a given dispute. We know interests to be the needs, concerns, desires, and even fears that people have. They underlie the positions people take and the specific things people argue that they want. They usually encompass the WHY and not the WHAT of a situation.

In a labor negotiation, the union may be seeking extra vacation days for its members while management is concerned about what seems to be lower productivity on the production line. What may underlie the articulated concerns, however, may be a problem of extreme boredom of the line workers in doing endlessly repetitive tasks. This has been translated by the union into a demand for more vacation days—anything to escape the ennui. The real interest to be addressed, however, is how to make the line jobs more stimulating and thus increase productivity. If the true underlying interest is not addressed, the parties may "resolve" the positions taken but not the common problem. Whenever this occurs, the underlying problem will recur, perhaps in another guise, and the parties will again face conflict.

In a family dispute, the husband and wife are seen endlessly at war over whether their son should be in a public or a private school. Reasonable arguments are advanced for the contending points of view (cost, diversity, class size, supporting public schools, etc.) If, however, Dad's real issue is that Dad wants his son to have access to a good football program while Mom's real issue is that she wants him to get a religious education, all the cogent arguments pro and con about public and private schools will be irrelevant.

Where a patient has threatened suit against his physician for malpractice over a relatively minor matter, it often turns out that what the patient really wants is an acknowledgment by his doctor that he, the patient, is a man, not a number on a case file, and that the doctor is capable of error. An apology can end a malpractice suit.

Conflicts are not limited to purely interest-based matters. They may encompass interests, rights, and power all at the same time. This is typically the case in disputes over political matters involving states. The discussions over the status of political boundaries, nationhood, and peoples will have aspects of all three methods of resolution. However, where there is an acknowledgment by the parties that they have a joint problem to be solved, the most useful technique to turn the parties away from war will be to concentrate on the interests of the parties, turning them away from positional bargaining, and toward joint problem solving.

CHAPTER TWO:
FORMS OF ALTERNATIVE DISPUTE RESOLUTION

In disputes of every kind, disputants and attorneys often turn quickly to litigation to determine "right and wrong" or "justice." Unfortunately, due to delays in getting to trial, extensive and expensive formal discovery processes, and the unpredictability of the jury system, litigation does not always provide a satisfactory resolution. Alternatives have always existed (from seeking the advice of a wise elder to hiring an expert and agreeing to be bound by her decision), but it is only recently in the United States that *alternative dispute resolution* (ADR) has become an understood and sought after alternative to litigation.

ADR is a term lightly used and rarely understood. It encompasses all forms of dispute resolution which are not litigation. Commonly used, it refers mostly to mediation and arbitration, which are discussed in detail later. Better defined, it is a lawyer or businessperson's toolbox, containing all the tools necessary to resolve disputes in the manner best suited to the dispute. Understanding what each tool is and how it works is essential to handle disputes effectively. Just as in a real toolbox, there will be some tools we use often and some used only for special projects. Some people will use a hammer for certain tasks while others might choose a mallet. Neither is right or wrong; the choice comes from familiarity, comfort, and the way each of us thinks through problems and chooses to solve them. The key is having all the necessary tools in your toolbox and knowing how to use them. Below we describe many of the tools available for dispute resolution. It will be apparent, however, that there are many more that can be forged or borrowed to fit each particular problem.

There are numerous reasons that people turn to ADR rather than litigation. First is time. Usually, it is quicker to choose almost any method of ADR than to go through the prolonged court process, especially where appeal is likely. Next is cost. Litigation is extremely expensive. Companies lose employee time attending hearings, depositions, and, finally, trial. Companies also lose employee concentration and good will when they are involved in a dispute with other employees or one that will affect the lives or livelihood of the employees. And, of course, attorneys fees and general litigation-related expenses can become prohibitive. Finally, parties choose ADR in order to maintain control over their dispute. Through ADR they can control who makes decisions, when, and how.

A study was conducted of ADR use by Assistant United States Attorneys (AUSA's) during a five-year period.[1] The study, released in 2000, revealed that ADR was successful in settling almost two-thirds (63 percent) of the cases where it was used and adding value in an additional 17 percent of the cases. Benefits other than settling included gaining insight into plaintiff's case, preventing future disputes, and narrowing the issues in the case. And while the average cost of mediation was $867 and a total of nineteen hours was spent preparing for or attending a mediation session, AUSA's estimated that they saved $10,700 in litigation costs, eighty-nine hours of staff time (legal, paralegal, administrative time), and six months of litigation time.[2] The study further concluded that it was most effective to use ADR voluntarily rather than when ordered by a court, and that, while cases were far more likely to settle closer to trial, the cost savings was far greater if ADR was used early in the litigation process.[3]

The Toro Corporation is also a strong proponent of ADR, including early intervention/negotiation and mediation very early in the dispute. Through its program, after six years, it has reduced the cost of handling each claim by an average of $45,600 per claim, with payouts reduced by 73 percent and insurance premiums reduced by an average of $1.8 million per year. Toro estimates its savings at over $50 million, and that

---

1. Jeffrey M. Senger, "Evaluation of ADR in United States Attorney Cases," *United States Attorneys' Bulletin*, Nov. 2000 at p. 26. It appears that the study almost exclusively discusses mediation as opposed to all forms of ADR.

2. *Id.*

3. *Id.* at p. 27.

does not quantify increased customer satisfaction due to reduced time to resolve disputes and increased individualized attention to each client's concerns.[4]

There are no limits to the forms of alternative dispute resolution that exist or may be created. There are, however, a number of commonly used and recognized forms which range from very informal to quite formal. Some forms are court-annexed, that is, in some manner supervised by a court in which an action has been commenced in the matter. Some forms proceed solely by agreement of the parties and are completely independent of the courts. It is useful to understand these commonly used forms of ADR so you are able to decide which form will work in each particular dispute, modify it as necessary, and design an ADR process that works best.

NEGOTIATION

The most informal resolution device is conversation between or among the parties in which each party tries to persuade the other of a certain viewpoint as they work together to find an acceptable compromise. Negotiation may be as simple as which movie to see on Friday night or as complex as the Israeli-Palestinian conflict. The parties may or may not enlist the services of legal or other counsel in order to engage in negotiation. If success is to crown their efforts, the talks must be conciliatory. The hope of reaching consensus is what turns conversation into negotiation. These talks may move to another stage of dispute resolution when the parties and/or counsel believe that the intervention of a neutral would be useful in moving the negotiations.

Negotiation is also the basis for most forms of dispute resolution. Even where someone else is deciding the outcome, negotiation is used in choosing the decision-maker, setting rules for discovery and introduction of evidence, and in setting out

---

4. Upchurch, John, "Pre-Litigation Resolution of Claims through Early Intervention/Mediation," *The Revolutionizing Litigation Management Report*, (June 1995); followed up by Olivella, Miguel A., Jr., "Toro's Early Intervention Program, After Six Years, Has Saved $50 M," *Alternatives* (April 1999).

the rules the decision-maker must follow in coming up with the decision. Strong negotiation skills are essential to make alternative dispute resolution successful.

MEDIATION

Mediation is a process by which the parties enlist the aid of a neutral third party to facilitate a negotiation to resolve their joint problem. The role of the mediator is to assist the parties in understanding the nature of the problem, the underlying interests of all parties, and the various options that may exist which can help resolve all, or part, of the problem. The mediator's job is to facilitate. The resolution of the problem must be one that the parties have either created themselves or, at least, believe in as a solution. Where various interests underlie the conflict, the mediator must find them and, where appropriate, suggest options that trade off the underlying interests so each party will be satisfied that he has obtained a fair result. That fairness must be felt. The substantive outcome must be acceptable psychologically for the conflict truly to end.

Mediation, which emphasizes interest-based bargaining, is, after negotiation, the method of conflict resolution with the lowest transaction costs. It involves a minimum of stress and consumes relatively little time and money. But not every conflict should be mediated. Where the parties are not prepared to settle, mediation likely will not be successful. Thus, if the parties are at a stage where their knowledge of the facts is minimal, mediation may be helpful to show them what they need to learn but it will not immediately resolve the conflict.

Where one or both parties believe that a precedent must be set, mediation again is the wrong device for resolution. Mediation between private parties always involves rigid confidentiality and is of limited application. Thus, where the issue involves whether children, without regard to ethnic background, should attend the same schools, mediation could resolve the immediate conflict but not become the basis for a constitutional precedent. Only adjudication in a court of competent jurisdiction can accomplish that aim. Similarly, where one party to an industry-wide contract wants an authoritative decision on the meaning of a particular clause in the agreement to be applied in all cases, the courtroom is the place to resolve that issue. If the entire industry is bound by an arbitration clause, the same result may occur. For the setting of important precedents, arbitration usually lacks the right to appeal, the safeguard that is most necessary for precedent setting.

In the study conducted by the Assistant United States Attorneys, a variety of advantages were gained by using mediation:

> "Mediation helped patch up an employee/employer relationship, preventing other foreseeable disputes."

> "The settlement was better and more carefully designed than what a court could have ordered."

> "[Mediation] . . . encouraged the agency to realize the actual risks of trial."[5]

For parties who wish to maintain control over the outcome of their dispute, or have a future relationship at stake, mediation usually is the ideal alternative.

ARBITRATION

Other than mediation, the most widely used ADR device is arbitration. Some industries have arbitration clauses in their contracts. Principally, the securities and construction industries seek to resolve disputes in this format.

Like mediation, arbitration is established by contract among the parties. Unlike mediation, where the mediator is not a decision-maker, the arbitrator or panel of arbitrators usually reaches a conclusion that is binding on the parties and not subject to appeal. The power of the arbitrator(s), however, is set by the contract.

---

5. Senger, *supra* note 1, at p. 28.

Procedure for an arbitration is usually much less formal than at a trial. The rules of evidence are not scrupulously applied. Binding arbitration, sometimes called "winner take all," is usually inexpensive and not especially time-consuming. Frequently, as compared with adjudication through litigation, arbitration justifies the efforts of the makers of the contract in keeping transaction costs low. However, there has been an erosion of this goal, particularly in large commercial cases. Attorneys for the parties have insisted that the arbitrator(s) grant liberal discovery just as in a court of law. Where the arbitrator(s) has done so, the transaction costs have skyrocketed and the benefits of arbitration as a low cost ADR device have plunged.

Many courts provide for court-annexed or nonbinding arbitrations. Under this plan, the parties present their arguments in truncated fashion to the arbitrator(s). An advisory ruling is forthcoming which informs but does not bind the parties. In the "Michigan Mediation" form, the arbitrators attempt to mediate the dispute after reaching their conclusion.

The nonbinding ruling is really a form of another ADR device, the Early Neutral Case Evaluation. Neutral Evaluation is discussed at length in chapter 5. If the parties have confidence in the person(s) serving as the arbitrator(s), the advisory ruling may form the basis of settlement negotiations, which will resolve the case. If that confidence is lacking, the parties will ignore the advice and proceed with their lawsuit.

NEUTRAL EVALUATION AND EXPERT FACT FINDING

Neutral Evaluation

Neutral evaluation, often referred to as *early neutral evaluation*, may be used by itself or in conjunction with mediation. In neutral evaluation, a trained neutral, usually with experience in the subject matter of the dispute, hears arguments from both sides and sometimes is presented with an important witness's testimony or documentary evidence in support of both sides. The neutral then provides an opinion as to the probable outcome of the dispute in court, and often offers a suggested settlement option. Some neutral evaluators take the parties aside and point out the strengths and weaknesses of the case. Others, upon providing their opinion, will try to guide the parties toward a resolution. They have no authority to tell the parties what to do. The argument against a neutral evaluator switching hats to mediation is that she has already taken a side in the negotiation and her neutrality may be compromised.

Expert Fact Finding

Occasionally, the parties need the assistance of a neutral fact finder to assist the process. Where disputed facts and particularly disputed matters involving expertise are involved, the parties may agree to retain someone who will investigate and report back to them. This may be part of a larger mediation proceeding or independent of it. Sometimes the neutral fact finder actually serves as a co-mediator in the mediation.

OTHER FORMS

One well known form of ADR is the court-sponsored *settlement week*. In this widely used approach, the local bar supplies personnel to sit with the parties and help them reach a settlement. The court staff, by various means, determines which cases are to be included. Ordinarily, these will be cases in which discovery has been completed and which are ready for trial. No fixed rules attend the process by which the volunteer lawyer aids the parties. If the lawyer is a skilled mediator she may use those skills. More often, however, the lawyer will endeavor to do what she thinks the judge would do at a pretrial settlement conference. The tactics would include some form of case evaluation, prediction of likely outcome, review of costs of not settling, and so forth.

Court-supervised *summary jury trials* are still another form of ADR. In this format, the judge actually presiding in the case works with counsel and clients to reach a settlement. This form of ADR works best in cases where the predictions of the parties as to the likely outcome are very far apart. The court summons one or more jury panels to the courtroom. Counsel, in the presence of their clients, present arguments to these panels based on the evidence adduced in discovery. The panels then deliberate and advise the court and the parties as to how they would resolve the matter. The effort frequently aids in settlement, particularly where the jury "verdicts" inject reality into the parties' own deliberations.

The *mini trial* is a form of ADR which can be done with or without the supervision of the judge. Most often it is arranged privately by counsel. Here the clients and some witnesses attend the "trial." Often, the clients are the "jury" and hear presentations of the adversary evidence and theory for the first time, unfiltered by their own counsel. Usually the party representatives are executives from the companies who were not personally involved with the dispute and who have authority to resolve the matter on behalf of the company. The case is presented in summary fashion. Questioning of some witnesses, particularly experts, is done. Counsel can be questioned by the clients. In fact, the procedure is whatever the parties want. Although the judge is rarely involved in this form of ADR, it is usually a good idea to have some neutral facilitator present to help administer the proceeding. Negotiations among the parties, perhaps mediation, ordinarily follow the holding of the mini trial.

Rent-a-judge, a procedure widely used in California, has spread to other states. Retired judges are retained by the parties and a trial is held pursuant to rules fashioned by the parties. The courts are bypassed, the parties agreeing by contract to abide by the results. Unlike arbitration, in private judge trials, the parties usually insist on all the formalities observed in a court of law, including the application of the rules of evidence. In California, there is some provision for appeals. In other jurisdictions, there is no appeal from the decision of the private judge.

In addition, there are a number of variations on mediation and arbitration. These are discussed in more detail in chapter 13.

CHAPTER THREE:
THE DYNAMICS OF CONFLICT

OVERVIEW

The strategy to be used in resolving conflict depends upon its source. For example, conflicts may be generated by a falling out among business partners, each insisting upon more of the business than the other deems acceptable during dissolution of the company. To the extent that the disagreement is substantive, related only to the articulated disagreement over the appropriate split of assets and business, the parties will be most successful when they recognize that they are business people who have a business problem that they must resolve together.

It is almost never that simple, however. The underlying feelings that generated the conflict in the first place will get in the way of rational discussion. It is the relational problem that gave rise to what is now a business problem laced with heated emotion, blame, and guilt. This type of situation is not uncommon. The underlying anger sends people to the courthouse. Oddly, years later, when the former partners finally get to face each other at trial, the weight of the passage of time, the enormous expense of the litigation, and the stress associated with it will likely reduce the original anger to fatigue. Settlement on the courthouse steps, achieved in over 90 percent of all civil cases, likely will occur in this situation as well.

If the parties had been brought together early in the conflict and given an opportunity to vent their frustrations and emotions, the heat might have been reduced sufficiently for them to have seen that what was left to do was to solve their mutual business problem. In short, if the parties are able to get past the emotions, find the true underlying interests often masked by the positions they take, and understand the nature of the joint problem to be solved, they are well on the way to resolution. Once on the road to joint problem solving, the dispute will likely be settled quickly and fairly.

Since what appears on the surface is almost always driven by something lurking beneath, however, it seems wise to pause briefly and recognize the kinds of things that create unnecessary conflict and erect barriers to successful resolution.

EMOTIONS

Most conflicts have a strong emotional base. These emotions or feelings are often the true basis of the conflict. Unless they are uncovered, acknowledged, and understood, the parties are not likely to be able to resolve their difficulties on their own or with the aid of a neutral. The emotional base usually results in an attempt by the parties to resolve their conflict through the use of power together with an attempt to vindicate rights.

The causes of emotional underpinning to conflict are as numerous and manifold as the conflicts they spawn. They may be personal, stemming from a marriage or other familial relationship. They may be relational in the sense of business or acquaintance. In virtually all relational-based conflict, the causes are deeply rooted in perceived behavioral problems coupled with poor communications and misperceptions between the now warring parties. It is not possible to pull apart all the incidents of apparent indignity that have brought the parties to their present unhappy pass. It will be enough just to have them acknowledge their feelings sufficiently to put them on a path of mutual resolution, putting their mutual resentment behind them, or at least away for another day.

COMMUNICATION PROBLEMS AND MISPERCEPTION

A related aspect of relational conflict, indeed of most interpersonal conflict, is misperception based on a lack of communication. The failure of communication may be the result of a sullen dislike for the individual. In the alternative, it may be that these parties have never communicated effectively. They may come from different cultural backgrounds and have been unable to "hear" each other. As a result of differing ethnic or cultural heritages, they may not "understand" what they hear. As a result of negative stereotyping they may never have wanted to communicate.

The illustrations of these failures to communicate are all around us. If we take the instances of communication failures among Israelis and Arabs, Serbs and Croats, blacks and whites, men and women, we have just begun to see the magnitude of the problem. The Israelis and their neighbors the Palestinians still cannot agree on the shape of the table after almost fifty years of war and lack of communication.

Just because the case before you involves a salesman seeking commissions from his employer, one cannot blithely assume that these folks know how to talk to each other. Indeed, it cannot be assumed that they have ever really talked to each other. A "boss" giving orders to a subordinate may be as close to communication as these people have ever been. They must TALK TO EACH OTHER if their problem is to be solved in their mutual interest.

ROLE PROBLEMS

The structure in which the conflict arose and in which it must be resolved often affects the manner in which the parties view the conflict and the procedures needed to resolve it. An understanding of the roles played by each party is essential. If the opposing parties will have to work together as employee and employer, it is essential that an agreement recognize the underlying interests and the reality of the relationship, permitting the parties to work together in the future. If the need is for an agreement to solve an urgent problem, the agreement can be fashioned to leave other issues open for later negotiation. The nature of the relationship may call for an agreement that creates a procedure for the resolution of future disputes.

Role or structural disputes frequently involve unequal power or resource allocations among the parties. These issues are complex and varied. They are discussed in more detail in chapter 6, in the context of mediation.

INFORMATIONAL PROBLEMS

Although emotional problems underpin most disputes, there are a substantial number that have been created or will be unyielding because of misinformation or lack of information. These are sometimes called "data conflicts." They stem from a lack of information or from plain misinformation. Any lawsuit that moves to the discovery phase illustrates the point. Counsel, in an attempt to protect the client, complies with discovery requests and orders as narrowly as seems appropriate under the circumstances. Yet counsel's view of what ought to be relevant is seldom the same as his adversary's view. Even though relevance is not necessarily the standard of discovery, most informational problems that arise after initiation of the action stem from varying concepts of relevance. The action itself may have begun, in part, from the refusal of one party to share information with the other. Had disclosure been made in informal conciliatory conversations, the lawsuit might have been avoided. The specter of physicians refusing to share the patient's own file with the patient and his representative is a simple example of how lack of information can provoke avoidable conflict. In the corporate field, the refusal to make disclosure to shareholders or joint venturers fuels fires.

Conflict comes in many forms and its causes are too numerous even to contemplate. In searching for solutions, however, it is necessary to have some understanding of the basis for the conflict. That understanding will help us define issues and move forward toward solving the problem.

CHAPTER FOUR:
NEGOTIATION

OVERVIEW

The most commonly used form of dispute resolution is the process of negotiation. Where there is a disagreement between or among two or more people or organizations, we usually attempt to resolve our differences through some form of give-and-take discussion before resorting to more formal, and expensive, means of determining an outcome. War is not a form of negotiation, though some negotiators believe otherwise. The fact that one party comes away from a negotiation satisfied with the outcome is not an indicia of success—except in the limited WIN-LOSE sense. In the truly successful negotiation both parties come away persuaded that the problem has been resolved to their mutual satisfaction. They are satisfied with the substance of the agreement and feel that they have been treated properly. This psychological satisfaction is important if the agreement is actually going to be carried out and/or if there is a continuing relationship among the parties. This is the WIN-WIN concept of interest-based bargaining.

Though we tend not to think about it, we engage in forms of negotiation almost every day. If we want our spouse to come along to a film we wish to see, but he or she does not, we engage in some give-and-take conversation. If, on the other hand, the tactics we use to coerce the unfortunate mate involve the assertion of power or guilt or threats, the relationship will be an unhappy one, however brief its duration. We may get to see the film but the cost may be very great indeed. If the parties do not understand the dynamics of this little scenario, if their underlying interests are masked in the haggling over their positions, we likely will have a LOSE-LOSE ending.

NEGOTIATING EFFECTIVELY REQUIRES GOOD COMMUNICATION SKILLS

One of our colleagues holds that "The first casualty of conflict is communication."[6] When there are problems, people forget how to talk them out or simply refuse to try. We get too involved personally, whether we are trying to figure out what toppings to put on a pizza, handling the merger of two multibillion dollar companies, or resolving highly controversial litigation. The first step is to communicate. It may be as simple as making it clear to the friend who is ordering the pizza that you cannot **stand** anchovies rather than making your statement vague enough to imply that it's okay to order them and you will pick them off. We can already visualize the argument when the pizza arrives—who was right and who was wrong? Can we resolve even this simple conflict if the parties get mad at each other and stalk out of the house? Perhaps the hardest part of negotiating is finding a way to restore or to begin effective communication.

Understanding

Few people are truly effective communicators. Too often arguments occur simply because people misunderstood each other, or interpreted a statement differently than it was meant. It is easy to see how such miscommunication leads to conflict. It is also important to see that miscommunication can ruin negotiations or at least complicate them. Knowing how to convey information clearly and how to ensure that you understand information provided by others is essential. Fortunately, most of the skills required for good communication are skills we already know or at least have heard of. Unfortunately, using these skills effectively requires frequent practice. The first step in communicating, then, is understanding. After understanding we can turn to persuading and the natural give-and-take of negotiation.

---

6. Raytheon Rawls, vice president, Resolution Resources Corporation.

In the field of alternative dispute resolution, understanding is accomplished through a group of skills gathered under the heading of *active listening.* Active listening means listening so the other party knows that you are really hearing him, that you understand what he is saying, and that you can see the positive side of what he has said.[7] Keep in mind that understanding and acting on what you hear do not mean that you necessarily agree with or will comply with the party's statements and demands. It simply means that you will make a real effort to see this issue from his perspective and will take that point of view into account when you act. From an interest-based bargaining perspective, it means that your offer will consider the other party's needs and interests as well as your own.

How do we listen effectively?

- Make eye contact.
- Give physical attention (body language conveys listening).
- Ask open-ended questions.
- Reflect on what is being said.

People want to know that they are being heard. Making eye contact lets them know that you are interested. Wandering or downcast eyes, in our culture, implies that you are not listening.[8] Turning your whole body toward the talker also helps people know that you are involved in the conversation. By giving them your whole attention, not only does it make them feel good, but it helps you gain greater insight than you would if you were listening with half your brain and thinking about your response with the other half.

---

7. R. Fisher, W. Ury, *Getting to Yes, Negotiating Agreement Without Giving In,* (Penguin Books 1991) pp. 34–35.

8. In other cultures, however, making eye contact may be taken as disrespect or even as a threat. If you are not sure, follow the cues or ask. People generally are pleased to know that you are interested enough to raise the question.

Studies have shown that about 85 percent of communication is nonverbal.[9] Thus, by watching and listening, we are more likely to get all of what people are saying. When a child says "I'm not tired," we look to see whether he is rubbing his eyes. When a spouse says "I don't mind if you go out with your friends," we look to see whether she is crossing her arms or frowning. The same is true in negotiation. Nervous gestures may give away lies or demands people know are outrageous and do not expect to meet. Closed gestures (arms folded, turning away, frowns) may indicate that you have a long way to go before you are ready to start talking about offers.

Now that you are paying attention, how do you make sure people talk? And that you understand what they're saying? *"One of the primary tasks of a listener is to stay out of the other's way so the listener can discover how the speaker views his situation."* [10] This means that we may start a conversation, but when we are truly trying to understand, we should not take charge of and direct that conversation. We accomplish this seemingly impossible task through the use of open-ended questions and reflective listening. Both skills sound extremely "touchy-feely," which usually scare lawyers and business people away. Fortunately, once mastered, both skills can be used without anyone having to come across as "soft."

Open-Ended Questions

Open-ended questions are those questions that encourage the respondent to answer fully and in the way they feel best answers the question. These questions, while providing some guidance, do not tell the respondent what kind of answer the questioning party is looking for. Open-ended questions may also be called

---

9. Robert Bolton, *People Skills*, p. 39 (Simon & Schuster, Inc. 1979).

10. *Id.* at p. 40.

"Newspaper Questions" or "Reporter's Questions." They generally start with "What," "When," "Where," "Why," and "How." Some examples of open-ended questions are:

- "What issues are at the heart of this dispute?"
- "When would your suggested solution work best?"
- "Where will you find evidence to support your theory?"
- "Why do you think the other side has taken that position?"
- "How can we create an offer that considers your need for closure and their need to delay payment?"

These same words can be used to conduct a closed and lawyerly directed examination, so working with the questions and trying to keep them open are essential. Some examples of how these questions might be used to conduct a direct examination are:

- "What did you do next?"
- "When can you wire us the money?"
- "Where did you get that?"
- "Why don't you just pay up and get it over with?"
- "How can you expect us to do that?"

Some of these questions may sound like open-ended questions, but they really are not looking for complete answers. The "What" question is the one lawyers use most. It walks us through a carefully directed discussion. It is highly effective in a courtroom, where you want to limit what the jury hears only to what you expect to be said. But in a negotiation, where more information will be more useful than less, such an examination is harmful rather than helpful.

Often, by really listening, and by asking the right questions, we find that the other side is not really unreasonable, or does not see things so differently than we do. Or we learn that his priorities *are* different from ours and it is easy to meet his interests while he meets ours. For example, in a sexual discrimination case, the company usually wants desperately to keep quiet the fact that it is being sued. It may appear that the plaintiff's main interest is to trumpet news of the company's wrongdoing to the world. Often it turns out that the employee really wants an apology and the reassurance that this action will not happen to anyone else. Armed with that knowledge, there are numerous ways to meet everyone's interests.

Using open-ended questions seems stilted and difficult at first. There are several techniques for practicing using them so they become more comfortable and genuine. One is to use them at home. "You say you don't want to stay home tonight? What were you thinking about doing instead?" rather than "You want to go out? Let's go to a movie." The other is to think of some questions that might be appropriate in a particular negotiation and jot them down. That way, when it becomes apparent that there is more information to be gleaned from the conversation and you are not sure how to gather it, you will have some questions prepared. For example, in a harassment lawsuit, the defense should make sure he possesses all the information that plaintiff has in order to assess liability and damages. Even if discovery is complete, there may be more information left outstanding. Some questions that might prove helpful throughout the negotiation include:

- "How will your witnesses describe the incident in question?"
- "How will you rebut our witness who watched the whole thing and will testify that no such actions took place?"
- "Who would you say is your strongest witness and why?"
- "What are your damage claims based on?"
- "Where would you like us to consider moving your client within the company?"

The understanding phase should continue until you really feel that you can see this problem from the other party's perspective and that you have enough information to evaluate your perspective fully. Be careful not to spend so much time questioning that you take over the discussion. Brief, well-phrased questions should open the door far enough to encourage the other party to provide information.

Reflecting

Once you think you truly understand the other party's side, it is time to double-check. We do this by reflecting on what we heard. Here is where most people think active listening gets too "touchy-feely." Not true at all. For those who like touchy-feely, reflecting is a great way to use those skills. For those who do not, they can still reflect effectively without ever uttering a touchy-feely phrase. Keep in mind, though, that what is important is what *they*, the hearers, will be most comfortable with, not you. If you want to win them to your side, or at least work well together, you have to make them understand that you are listening and struggling to comprehend.

Some touchy-feely reflecting phrases might include:

- "It sounds like you feel very sad about this divorce."
- "I hear a tone of frustration about this problem."
- "I can feel your anger."

Some non-touchy-feely phrases might sound more like:

- "This problem has really gotten in the way of your daily operations."
- "Let me make sure I understand the problem as you see it—first, you say this problem is interfering with your ability to do your work; second, you don't think you can continue working with Mr. X; and third, you say this problem has cost money in terms of counseling bills and legal fees. Did I miss anything?"
- "I think I see this issue from your point of view. Thank you. If you don't mind, I have a few questions to clarify what you said." Then use open-ended questions for that clarification.

Both approaches accomplish the same end—to make the other person understand that you were listening closely and thinking about what was said, and to make sure for yourself that you got it right so that you do not have miscommunication problems throughout the negotiation. Another, less obvious goal is also met—to help everyone else in the room hear the party's statement of feelings, interests, needs, and perceived facts without any inflammatory language.

While you are reflecting, it is important to take out the inflammatory language and boil it down to the feelings underlying the problem or the facts stated. The problem as you are reframing it can now be stated constructively (as a joint issue to be resolved) rather than negatively. All the blame and hurt can be left aside while the message is still heard. If one party says "That so-and-so harassed me and made it impossible to do my work. I can't even go into work without feeling humiliated," your reflection could be as simple as "I can see that this situation has made you very uncomfortable." You could follow up with a little more guiding question to get the party away from name-calling and anger: "Please tell me a little more about how your work has been affected."

This type of listening is especially helpful when the other party has strong feelings that need to be addressed before he will be ready to solve the problem. Quite often, just knowing that he was heard is enough to help him calm down and move on. But it must be genuine. "I see you are angry about this" in a sarcastic tone or even a monotone usually does not help. "Wow, I didn't realize how angry you were" might be more helpful. Or "Let me make sure I understand exactly why you are so angry—you say you are trying your best and being rejected because of your relationship with your boss; you feel that we, the management, have not done enough; and you are frustrated because you like your job and feel you cannot do it in this environment." After some amount of such careful listening and responding, even the angriest people usually calm down. The calmer you are, the more likely they are to respond. Of course, negotiation may not be effective for those who will never calm down enough to work out their troubles. There may be too much need for vindication, which many people perceive as being achieved only in a court of law.

In a situation where the other party is very angry or emotional, keeping your own anger and defensive feelings in check can be a very valuable negotiating tool. Instead of worrying about how you will defend yourself at the end of the tirade, concentrate on what he is saying. Think about why he would say it (use clarifying questions if necessary). Then reflect what you heard so you are sure you understood. Take out the anger and boil the statement down into feelings and interests ("It sounds like your being taken off that team when you feel ready to finish your project really has you worried"). Finally, note your disagreement and, when appropriate, use your information-conveying skills to counter the argument productively rather than defensively.

Reflective responses also help people stop rambling and prepare to move on. For one who keeps restating the problem in ever increasing detail, it is usually helpful to say something to the effect of "I think I see how this problem affects you; let's move on to discuss what can be done to resolve it." The hard part is figuring out when the party is ready to stop discussion and move forward to problem solving or even to listening to your perspective.

Reflective responses are also very useful in a dialogue. For example, where you have been listening to someone explain his needs and interests, it is often helpful to say "I didn't understand before that staying with the company is so important to you. We also want you to stay. Your skills at X, Y, and Z are important to us. The problem we have, then, is how to keep you with the company and avoid these issues in the future. Let's see what we can figure out." With one simple statement you have made the other party feel heard, expressed your own very specific interests, ended discussions of past wrongs and begun discussions of future good, and turned everybody from adversarial negotiation to joint problem solving. With practice, using this reflecting skill can have that effect more often than you would think.

Reflecting is equally important before you change topics or act on the topic you are discussing. "Before we go on, let's clarify what we've agreed on. While we take a break, you are going to find those documents. I will review them, then we'll meet again and work on the issue of . . ." In a mediation, reflecting is especially important in a confidential caucus (*see* chapter 6). "I need to go speak with the other party now. Let me make sure what is okay for me to reveal from our discussions here."

Robert Bolton emphasizes that reflecting is inappropriate in several instances, too.[11] When you simply cannot be genuine in your reflections, you should not try them. If they would come out sarcastic, judgmental, or dictatorial ("sounds like you need to do X"), try something simpler, like "I understand," or "Um hmm." And when you want to take over the problem and solve it yourself, reflecting also will not be helpful. "How could you get yourself into this mess?" is not a particularly helpful reflecting statement. In addition, restating repetitively can be just as bad as not restating at all. If you restate everything you hear, the listener will soon begin to feel that you are condescending or simply using tricks to make him like you. The response will be anger and frustration for all.

Conveying Information

Once you have heard the other party, it probably is best to make sure that he, too, has enough information and understanding on which to base a reasonable decision. We all know how to tell someone what we want and need, but doing it in a way that the person is able to hear it, and act on it, is harder than we think. People are so worried about how they will respond to what you say that they rarely listen as closely as we want them to. With children, it is possible to ask them to repeat what you have said in order to make sure they were listening. Not so with adults. By keeping our statements simple and clear, removing the blame and other phrases likely to cause defensiveness, and by repeating our statements as necessary, we stand a much better chance of being heard.

Especially in negotiation, tone is crucial. Strong, positive, in charge negotiators are much more likely to get what they want than are weak, tentative followers. It is much easier to convince people to see something from your perspective when you are positive and forceful in your explanation than when you are tentative. As a young mediator, the more tentative my tone, the

---

11. *Id.* at p. 109.

more likely the mediation was to fail. I found quickly that by convincing myself that I was quite capable, that confident demeanor translated immediately into confidence in me by the parties.

To help you feel as confident as you sound, there are a number of tools to use. First, of course, is preparation. Did you do your research? How will you convey your information to the other side? Do you have the cases with you? Do you have the comparable jury verdicts? What facts and figures will you show to convince the other side that you are right and that he should see it your way? Of course, if you just show up and stick your figures in front of people's noses and say "See? I'm right. Now let's do it my way," you are bound to lose unless your figures really are definitive and unarguable. There certainly are better ways to convey even the most convincing information.

First, keep your audience in mind. Are you negotiating with other experienced lawyers or is the real person you need to persuade a young, inexperienced, uneducated, and very timid person? Your language will change depending upon your audience. "Harassment" is a legal term that probably should not even be used when talking with lawyers because it is so vague. It certainly should not be used with nonlawyers, who are almost guaranteed to interpret the term differently than lawyers. Lawyers use legal terminology in everyday conversation, which most people do not understand. What's a "personal injury case"? What really does "preponderance of the evidence" mean? What do you want me to say in my "opening statement"? The first thing lawyers need to do in any negotiation where there are nonlawyers involved is to stop using legal terms. But make sure you do not lose track of who your audience is. Business people do not want their language too simplistic, either. This task seems so simple, but it can be tricky. What do you do when you have lawyers discussing legal issues among unsophisticated clients who really are going to make the decision on the resolution?

Next, keep in mind your goals. You are trying to convey *your* information and needs. This goal is often accomplished best by talking in terms of yourself. Many people are familiar with the term, *I statement*. It sounds like another touchy-feely phrase that will not work for most business people. On the contrary, it is an effective tool that works for everyone because it is really hard to argue with a statement like "I don't like that." You either get the childish response of "Yes you do" or, more likely, "Oh, I didn't know that." Using *I statements* is a persuasive way to state a feeling, need, or interest clearly and succinctly. For example, in response to a statement by one party that he is willing to offer only $20,000 in a case where liability is not at issue, it is hard to argue when the plaintiff states "I need $35,000 just to cover my medical bills." Assuming proper evidence of legitimate medical expenses, the initial offer should jump to $35,000. Then the parties can start talking about other needs and interests—attorney's fees, pain and suffering, lost wages, etc.

In a divorce case, where one party is going on and on about problems with the marriage, it might be very helpful for the other party to say something like "I feel very sad when we talk that way. To get past this, I need to think about positive things, like how we can work together to make sure the kids are happy." The speaker both expressed her emotions and turned the other party toward an issue that can be discussed and resolved rather than another rehashing of the problems. The key to using *I statements* is to avoid the use of "you." "You" is accusatory and puts people on the defensive. It is hard to have a reasonable conversation with someone who feels he has just been attacked. The same speaker could have said "You shouldn't talk that way. It makes me feel sad." The message is the same, but the listener rarely gets past "You shouldn't" without becoming more upset. Saying, "I need **you** to do X " sounds like an *I statement*, but it is not. It is a demand.

Finally, talk to persuade. Support your explanation of your needs and interests with reasons. "I need to see those financial statements before I go forward because I cannot create a budget and determine reasonable child support needs without them." "I am asking for an apology so that I can put this incident behind me." Persuade the other party with what lawyers refer to as *Demonstrative Evidence*. Bring a diagram or a video reenactment of the accident. That way, when you are discussing areas of disagreement about an accident, you have something to refer to. Bring a "Day in the Life" video of your client, who got hurt in the accident. It is one thing to talk about how the accident changed his life; it is quite another to show the defendant what a jury will see.

Respond to the other person's comments with efforts to find areas of commonality. "I understand that you disagree with my assessment of the situation. It is clear, though, that we both feel that we want to continue the relationship. So our task is to figure out how to work together and disagree constructively." Before you state your ideas, figure out how your suggestions will also meet the party's needs— "We both want this dispute behind us. I need to pay as little as possible up front; you need to pay your medical bills immediately. Let's see how we can work out a way to meet both of our needs."

Even disagreement can be stated constructively. "I understand that you feel that way. I need to explain why I feel differently." If your explanation is then full of reasons, nonthreatening language, and *I statements*, you should be well on your way toward resolution. Keep in mind, however, that in many instances, one round of listening and calm discussion is rarely enough. Usually it takes more reflective listening, more persuasive discussion, and more patience than you would wish in order to get the other party to turn toward joint problem solving.

Deciding What Information to Convey and When to Convey It

Only through experience can you become comfortable with knowing when and how much information to convey. Everyone has a different approach. Some people never convey anything unless forced to, on the theory that the less you know, the more likely they are to win. Others feel just the opposite: "Let the other party see what he would get through discovery anyway, so we can be working off the same page. I'll win brownie points for being generous and helpful, and the other side will actually have enough information on which to base a reasonable decision."

There are several issues to consider in deciding what information to provide:

- What information does the other party have?
- What more does he need in order to evaluate the situation effectively?
- Will it improve my chances of doing well in this negotiation if I provide this information?
- What effect will my revealing it have long term?
- If I provide this information, what can I expect to get in return?

Generally, people need enough information to evaluate the situation fairly and effectively. If a lack of information is causing miscommunications or misperceptions, then it is a fairly simple call to decide that you must provide the information to clear up the misunderstanding.

The decision becomes more complex when you possess a smoking gun that may or may not be revealed in discovery and that really will change the outcome in your favor. Most people would hide that smoking gun until trial. But what they are forgetting is that most cases are or can be resolved in negotiation, and especially in mediation. So if they want to use the smoking gun to "win" the dispute, negotiation is probably the ideal place to bring it out. A general rule might be that information that will help you move the other party closer to your point of view without overwhelming negative consequences should be revealed in a negotiation.

When to reveal information is another issue. Setting everything out right at the beginning rarely is effective. You do not know yet what the other party knows, what he thinks about what he knows, and what it will take to persuade him to your point of view. If you "fire all your guns at once," whether early or late, you lose the power of persuasion with each point. The key is to find the point during the discussions when your information will have the most impact. Is the other side ready to listen? Do you have supporting evidence or facts to back up your statement? Is this the point in the negotiation when the information will be most persuasive? If I provide this information now can I trade it for something useful ("I'll show you my financial statements if you show me yours"). There really are no bright line rules in making these decisions. You will have to consider each factor and weigh it carefully. With practice, it will become easier to make such decisions.

THE NEGOTIATION PROCESS

"In business, you don't get what you deserve, you get what you negotiate."[12] Negotiation is part of every dispute resolution process, and therefore must be understood and practiced in order to be used effectively. Even in arbitration and litigation, where someone else makes the ultimate decision, there are numerous issues to negotiate—what evidence will be introduced without the need for authenticating witnesses, when and where an arbitration will take place, how best to exchange information prior to a hearing, etc. While all these decisions can be made without good negotiation skills, having the skill to ensure that your needs and priorities are met in making those decisions can have a profound effect on the outcome. For example, if you know that a certain witness could make damaging statements if asked to testify, but is essential to establish authenticity of documents or a chain of custody of evidence, getting an agreement to waive the need for authenticating witnesses may be very important.

Preparation for Negotiation

Now that we have the basic skills to communicate in a negotiation, we are still not quite ready to enter the room and begin our negotiations. First we must prepare. While we all negotiate, few negotiate well. We all know people who always get a great deal on their house or car, find bargains everywhere they turn, and never pay full price for anything. We also know people who pay

---

12. Chester Karrass, *The Negotiating Game*, p. 3 (rev. ed. 1994).

asking price for everything. The bargain hunters are not lucky; they are prepared. And they are willing to take the steps necessary to negotiate the best agreement.

The first step to effective negotiation is preparation. Without it, you have no basis for negotiation. You cannot say, "Well, this car at ABC Dealership is $1,500 less," or "We must reject your offer of $50,000 because my medical bills are projected to be $45,000 and my attorneys fees are the same. The offer also does not cover pain and suffering, out of pocket expenses, work missed, etc. Here is how we value those items . . ."

First, you must do your research. What is it worth? What have juries done in comparable cases? How do those cases differ and what effect will that have? Why did the defendant make the offer we rejected? Are there objective standards upon which we can decide some or all of these issues? What issues are likely to arise—authority issues, relationship issues, time or cost constraints on the negotiation or solution, the effect on others of an agreement reached? How will I respond to the questions I can expect to be raised? Do I have enough information to make a decision? Do they? If not, how do we ensure that we all have sufficient and accurate information?

William Ury has set out five points for a mutually agreeable resolution that should be considered in preparing for any negotiation:

- Interests—intangible motivations that lead you to take certain positions;
- Options—possibilities for mutual gain that will satisfy some or all of each party's interests;
- Standards—independent measures of fair solutions (market value, laws, precedent);
- Alternatives—other ways of satisfying your interests without a negotiated agreement; and

- Proposals—possible agreements to which you are ready to say yes.[13]

Each point is considered in more detail below.

First, you must understand your own needs and interests. This includes evaluating your goals and prioritizing them. Most negotiating experts will tell you to set your aspirations high. Those who expect more will get more. No one will give you more than you ask for or expect.[14] Finally, you must understand your BATNA (Best Alternative to a Negotiated Agreement). This is your walk away point. If the offers cannot exceed your BATNA, you should be prepared to leave the negotiating table. BATNA, WATNA, and other methods for evaluating likely outcomes are discussed in detail in chapter 8.

Second, you must understand the other party's interests and needs. Who is he? What kind of negotiator is he going to be (positional, weak, tough but fair)? Why does he feel so strongly that his position is right? What needs of his will you have to meet so that he will walk away from this dispute? What interests will you need to meet to reach a resolution? What is his BATNA?

Third, search for objective standards by which the parties can agree to make decisions. In divorce cases, for example, states have guidelines for deciding how much child support should be paid. These standards set out factors to consider in reaching your decision. Actuarials in personal injury cases use tables to determine projected life span and lifetime income. In litigated claims, there are jury verdicts to use for comparison and contrast in determining a reasonable settlement figure.

Finally, you should explore some options and possible proposals. Ury considers options and proposals as separate entities.

---

13. Ury, *Getting Past No: Negotiating Your Way from Confrontation to Cooperation*, p. 16 (1991).

14. *Id.* at p. 25; Karrass, *supra* note 12 at p. 43.

Options are ways to meet interests. Proposals are agreements for resolving disputes.[15] Committing yourself to a particular option or proposal is rarely helpful, because things always arise during a negotiation that affect the outcome. But having some ideas for possible suggestions take some of the pressure off of you during the negotiation. Thinking about options in advance also allows you to consider how certain options meet your own needs and interests and to evaluate them from the other party's perspective. In this way you will be more comfortable with your negotiation.

At the least, you should think through what will have to be included in an agreement so that each important point is covered. Will you need to address interest, costs, or time of payments? What kind of release will be necessary? Are there related issues that should be resolved? In this way you are prepared to bargain on all important issues, which broadens the negotiation. It will also ensure that you will not reach the end of the negotiation and then remember an essential point that could change all the agreements reached.

Beginning the Negotiation

After participating in untold negotiations involving a wide variety of participants, it becomes clear that those participants who do best in negotiation approach it as a problem to be solved rather than as an adversarial confrontation. They greet everyone amicably, try to establish a positive tone in the room, and leave accusation out of the negotiation. While they are acting so amiably, however, truly effective negotiators are also guiding the negotiation toward resolution. After calming emotions and ensuring a positive tone, they then move to setting the agenda. They decide what to discuss first and how it will be discussed. This way, they are in control of the process. And this control helps them to lead the negotiation in the direction in which they wish it to go.

---

15. Ury, pp. 19–20; 24–25.

Most of us have been in a negotiation where we are presented with a preprepared form (a car or house sale, for example) and asked to sign it. Certain details are negotiable, such as the price and financing, but for the most part we do not question the rest of the form. This approach is like the negotiator who takes charge of the process—if everyone follows his lead, the basic form of the negotiation is already predetermined and the other participants become followers rather than leaders. Thinking through a possible agenda and taking a lead in the design and implementation of the process can have a significant impact on its outcome. Even if the entire agenda is not proposed initially, it can be helpful to have a mental image of what that agenda should be. That way, as one topic is covered, the next one is ready for consideration.

Exchanging Information

Once an agenda is set (flexible as it might and probably should be), the next step is to exchange information. As part of your preparation, you will have realized where you do not have sufficient information on which to base a decision. Other issues will arise throughout the negotiation, and you will need to dig for information before you respond. Bargaining should not take place until all parties feel confident that they understand the issues and have enough information to evaluate how suggested solutions will affect them. (When and how to convey information was discussed more fully in the discussion of communication skills, *supra*.)

Information should never simply be handed over. It should be presented, along with a strong argument for how each piece of information strengthens your case. And information should be received along with questions—what is the source of this information (the basis for its credibility)? What impact does it have on other information? Is there contradictory or supporting information? What exactly does this information mean in this case? Each question answered leads you closer to understanding the other party's interests, needs, strengths, and weaknesses.

How to Bargain in the Negotiation

Now that you are prepared for the negotiation, you must under-stand how to use the process to gain the best resolution possible. Sometimes negotiations resolve the entire dispute; other times they resolve only part of the dispute. In any event, making the process as effective as possible is essential. In order to make negotiation work, you should understand your own style of negotiation and decide which approach will work best in this particular dispute. Often we find that we change our approach to negotiation based upon the other party's approach. While this strategy can be effective in some cases, it may be more advantageous to help the other party see that your style is the best choice for this dispute.

POSITIONAL BARGAINING

When most people think about negotiations in the formal sense, they are most familiar with positional bargaining. This is a strat-egy of negotiation in which each side arrives at the table demanding some predetermined maximum, which they have no expectation of obtaining. Positional bargaining is reminis-cent of dealings with roadside vendors of curios in some underde-veloped countries. The initial demand for the trinket is $10.00. The haggling continues until, as the tourist threatens to drive off, the final price is reduced to $2.00, or whatever distress price the vendor believes will close the deal. In a negligence action, the plaintiff arrives at the table demanding $1,000,000 to settle her case while the defendant denies both liability and damages, and offers either zero dollars or something loosely called "nuisance value."

In many negotiations, one party arrives describing its position as nonnegotiable demands. In all positional bargaining, the nego-tiators view each other as adversaries. They see the outcome in terms of winners and losers. Quite naturally, each seeks to be the "winner," to have gotten the better of the bargain for himself or his client. The process is imbued with a large measure of ego. Each negotiator tends to believe, consistent with his ego invest-ment, that there is only one correct outcome: his. Since the rival camps view each other as the enemy, it is not surprising that the tactics in the negotiation tend to be based on concepts of power, secrecy, and manipulation rather than problem solving.

The negotiations then follow a similar pattern. The initial demand is extreme. The negotiators disclose as little information about their own or their client's true interests as is possible. The process goes on in relative ignorance laced by threats and bluffs from both sides. One side professes shock at the other's offer; the other threatens to leave the room. "Take it or leave it," is invariably heard, though rarely a true description of the negotiating position. "We'll let the jury decide," is a variant frequently uttered by the side that fears that body the most. The whole charade is filled with posturing, feigned anger, intimidation, and theatrics that have nothing to do with the problem that must be solved. Eventually, the parties will make small concessions to keep the process alive and to test how much movement there may be in the other side. It is a bit like trench warfare and about as effective. The game is hard on everyone involved. Tempers really do begin to flare. The process often hardens positions and renders problem solving more difficult. There is a pervasive fear in the negotiator that, if he "gives away too much," he will be seen as the loser.

How is anything ever resolved this way? Resolutions come when and if, after a series of small interim moves, the parties find themselves within the preplanned range of settlement. For instance, if plaintiff's original demand was $1,000,000 and defendant's nuisance cost $10,000, we would all agree that the parties are not likely to settle the case . . . unless these initial positions are known from the outset to be wildly artificial. If plaintiff's game plan calls for settlement in the range of $150,000–$300,000 and defendant's own secret agenda permits resolution in the $100,000–$150,000 range, the case will be settled if the bargainers do not destroy the negotiation by the manner in which they pursue it.

Why did the parties not disclose the settlement range in the first place? The way positional bargaining is played, the disclosure of the acceptable figure at the outset would not be believed. Even if counsel announced that this was the figure his client really would accept, his adversary would most likely treat the number as merely an opening gambit. The result would be an attempt to substantially whittle the amount down, however unrealistic. The negotiation would fail.

The lack of trust that attends positional bargaining is both a strength and a weakness. The strength is in the fact that settlements can occur without the need for trust. The weakness is that potentially attractive options and alternatives usually will not be explored because of the lack of shared information.

Where the negotiation takes place on the courthouse steps years after the onset of litigation and after all discovery has been completed, the process is altered because of the knowledge each party has acquired. The same posturing goes on, but in a more informed atmosphere. Since well over 90 percent of all civil cases are resolved prior to litigation, each party has the reasonable expectation that his case will settle at the eleventh hour. With the acquisition of needed data, the negotiations, though adversarial, are less likely to fail because of deceit. By the time the jury is being selected, the parties and counsel are well aware of the range of acceptable settlement amounts.

This comes, however, after years of battle. Why not settle either before the litigation or early in the process? Controversies involving parties with a continuing relationship of a commercial nature often do settle without litigation or early in the action. Cases where the parties' only interaction will be the lawsuit, as in the typical personal injury case, do not. Plaintiff's lawyers believe that the defendant's insurer will not settle until the very last moment. They believe the insurer will hold onto the money and earn interest on it for as long as possible. Defendant's counsel believes that the plaintiff has no interest in early settlement, preferring instead to try his luck with the jury, or in any event, await a better offer closer to the day of trial.

Interviews with plaintiffs' lawyers and insurance company executives indicate that these assumptions are questionable. The plaintiff who can settle her case in Year 1 for $200,000 but who waits until Year 5 may indeed get a larger offer, perhaps as much as $300,000. However, plaintiff's $200,000 in Year 1 is worth the same or more than the larger offer in Year 5. The plaintiff will have the money to invest and, even in times of low interest rates, there are many safe investments that will pay out the $100,000 or better. In addition to having the money earlier, the plaintiff will not have to face the years of trial preparation and uncertainty and stress. Counsel will, through earlier settlement, have less of an investment to make in each case and will recover the investment faster. The frequent cash flow problems of plaintiffs' lawyers would be lessened.

Many insurance companies have conducted studies of their own settlement tactics in connection with the advent of widespread mediation. The earlier settlement costs the insurance company significantly less than the one made as the jury is being sworn. Their studies show that the difference in settlement amount combined with the legal fees to be paid over the years is not canceled out by investment income on the reserves set aside to cover the claim. This is particularly true when their cost of borrowing for operations is taken into account. In short, many insurance companies have decided that it is in their financial interest to pursue earlier settlements.

THE MOVE TO INTEREST-BASED BARGAINING

It is perfectly understandable that where one party bargains positionally, the other party will respond with positional bargaining. This approach works best for negotiations where the parties truly do not care if no resolution is reached and are prepared to walk away. In most disputes, however, parties wish to find a resolution and put the dispute behind them. The most effective way to reach resolution is usually through *interest-based bargaining*. More and more attorneys are using this approach, and it is the basis for most mediations.

For *interest-based bargaining* to succeed there must be some mutual trust in the process. That can be established by the use of information that both parties believe is accurate. Instead of withholding information as in positional negotiating, the process depends upon the parties being open and the data being verifiable. The more information the parties have, the more likely the dispute will be settled on a basis that is acceptable to everyone involved.

In order to turn to *interest-based bargaining*, the negotiators (perhaps with the help of a mediator) must:

- Uncover the real interests and needs of the parties;
- Define the common (joint) problem(s); and
- Move the discussion to the joint solution(s).

A hypothetical situation that illustrates the need to move from positional bargaining to interest-based bargaining would involve two religious newspapers serving the same community. Say the parties had entered into an agreement several years earlier allowing Newspaper B to reprint any community service announcements printed in Newspaper A. Newspaper A has now sued Newspaper B, alleging that Newspaper B had greatly overstepped the bounds of the agreement and subsequently violated Newspaper A's copyright protection. Settlement negotiations have broken down because the parties are discussing only dollar figures to cover alleged but not easily quantifiable monetary damages. What the parties must understand is that the key to settling the dispute is to place the damage issue second, after exploring their common interests and the need to protect those interests through a joint resolution. For example, the parties must be concerned about their continuing relationship in the community, as well as how they can better serve the community without hurting their subscription rate or their perception in the community. By moving to interest-based bargaining, the parties can resolve the issue of damages because the parties will have an appropriate framework for discussion and will understand the need for joint problem solving.

The difference between joint problem solving and adversary position taking is striking. The huge investment in ego that is always associated with positional processes is unnecessary where all sides invest in trying to explore options that will lead to a solution. In theory, if the negotiators understand that their role is not to vindicate rights or win at the expense of an adversary, but instead to aid in fashioning a resolution that suits everyone, the ills of positioning fall away.

To accomplish this first goal of finding the real needs and interests, the negotiators must separate the people from the problem.

This means that the parties must see the substantive side of the problem separately from the relationship side. While the relationship side will need to be dealt with, it should not be mixed up with the substance of the dispute. By handling them together, they simply confuse the negotiation. The emotions which may underlie the dispute (and which counsel may have adopted) must be defused.

There are so many emotional issues in a negotiation—the history of the relationship between the parties, attitudes toward the concept of "justice" or "fairness," and how the attorneys have interacted with the parties (condescendingly, angrily, or respectfully). When you factor in unrelated problems at home that interfere with the ability to focus on this problem, ego problems such as how to face the boss if the negotiation is less than brilliant, and nervousness about negotiating ability, emotions become a strong element in most negotiations. Even where the parties are all business people and the problem is purely business, emotion can get in the way. Often it is enough to acknowledge the emotions and make it clear that you understand them.

When the parties are calm enough to discuss the problem, they can begin to focus on the problem and the related or underlying issues. The aim of interest-based bargaining is for the parties to generate a variety of options, which they will evaluate jointly. Both parties and their counsel will be looking for opportunities to satisfy underlying needs in a way that will bring permanent peace. The concept is WIN-WIN rather than WIN-LOSE. Both parties work for objectives that bring them substantive as well as psychological satisfaction.

The focus in *interest-based bargaining* is on the needs and interests of the parties rather than on the positions they take in the negotiation. Also, looking behind stated interests and finding the "real" ones might be essential to resolution. Here is where the *open-ended questions* become critical. "Why do you take that position?" "What do you base that demand on?" "What do you hope to accomplish today?" "Are you more interested in re-employment or a cash settlement?" "Why do you say you need X?" "How do you prioritize its importance compared with your other request for C?" Often, if the negotiators understand why the parties feel the way they do or make the demands they make, they find that there are ways to meet many of the needs of both parties and still resolve the problem. By discussing interests and needs, the parties also begin to prioritize their needs, seeing what is important to each other and finding areas in which they can compromise without feeling like they have "lost."

Exploring interests helps tremendously in the next step—defining the joint problem(s) and common interests. Simply understanding why the other party takes such an opposite view is important. If the parties also understand just how much they agree upon, resolution is much easier. It may be helpful to identify the issues the parties have in common and start the negotiation with those issues. Both employer and employee need to maintain their good relationship with the other employees. Both parents obviously want what is best for the children. The general contractor and bricklayer both want a finished product in which they can take pride. Jointly, then, they must consider how to reach that goal. With this approach, parties are no longer engaged in adversarial negotiations. They have turned toward joint problem solving. They have stopped looking backward to find and assign blame and have turned forward to search for ways to meet their goals.

After understanding the parties' interests and needs and defining the joint problem(s), it is time to start considering options in order to reach a joint solution. At this point it is easy to slip into positional bargaining again. One party comes up with a comprehensive proposal and cannot understand why the other party simply will not accept it. Instead of creating such proposals, it is better to start off by considering options. This is where all those options that were created during the preparation phase come into play. As options are considered, evaluated, and combined, proposals can be created from them.

More than one option should be generated for each issue. This can be done through brainstorming on every possible solution without evaluating any of them. Or the parties may simply throw out several options at once, noting that they are simply ideas that need to be considered and later refined. The options should each be designed for mutual gain. There should be give-and-take so that each option meets at least some of the needs of all parties. For example, an option could be that the visitation schedule have the children at each parent's house for alternating holidays—Christmas at Mom's but birthday at Dad's this year, and the opposite next year.

The generating of options by the parties, coupled with the sharing of information and interests, will often lead to an expansion of the range of settlement options—sometimes called expanding the pie. Narrow concepts of single payment settlements give way to structured settlements. Parties in business relationships find ways to expand rather than contract the relationship in order to meet their respective needs. Understanding that an ongoing relationship may require different options at different phases also helps parties move toward resolution; they realize they are not stuck with today's solution if they build in options for modifying the agreement as circumstances change.

After considering a number of options, the parties are more likely to be prepared to consider full proposals. For example, in a construction dispute, options might include discounted work on the ongoing project or on the next project already begun together in exchange for foregoing claims of negligence on the project at issue. After thinking through many of these possibilities, it is possible that the parties will choose one of them or simply decide that it will be best if some portion of payment due will be forfeited to compensate plaintiff for losses accumulated due to delayed work by defendant. With no acknowledgment of wrongdoing required in the agreement, the proposal might help the defendant "save face," that is, not have to admit he might have acted less than professionally, while at the same time allowing the plaintiff to "punish" him for delaying or costing plaintiff money on the project. Then any other claims can be addressed, with each solution either joined to or separated from the first issue. Options can then be combined to create comprehensive agreements, modifying them as needed to cover all parts of the problem.

In evaluating options and proposals, *interest-based bargaining* looks to objective criteria. Negotiators should look for a standard on which a decision can be based. These standards were explored during the parties' preparation for the negotiation, and should be raised as options and proposals are considered. Offering a choice of standards implies that a party has really thought through the problem and is making a strong effort to find a reasonable solution.

Working through these steps helps parties move from positions to interests, from stalemate to solution. Each time a party moves back to positional bargaining, probing questions and refusing to change negotiating tactics can move them back to *interest-based bargaining*. By exploring common interests and finding joint solutions, all parties "win" the negotiation.

Overcoming Barriers or Stumbling Blocks

There are numerous reasons that negotiations fail. Many of those reasons, if recognized, can be handled so that the negotiations can succeed. Some general tactics for getting a negotiation past an apparent barrier include:

- Taking a break;
- Restating areas of agreement (and perhaps disagreement);
- Breaking one issue into several smaller issues;
- Trading concessions ("I'll give you that letter of apology if you drop the fraud claim");
- Using humor;
- Brainstorming, together or separately;
- Helping the parties figure out a way to make concessions without losing face; and
- Creating doubt with questions like "What if we do that, and the result they think will happen really does?" or "Is there another way to meet your need to be more comfortable in your job other than the way you suggested?"

The basic idea is to shake up the discussions and get them off of the dead end they have followed. Find another path.

Differing Opinions on How to Interpret Data

Differences in the interpretation of data often separate the parties and send them off to a jury to decide the issue. The negotiator can ease this situation by working toward a common understanding of the data. Often it turns out that the differing interpretations are either not as far apart as they seemed initially, or can be brought together by clarifying questions to better understand each interpretation. This way, parties can clear up misunderstandings and often persuade one another of a jointly acceptable interpretation. Failing that, the negotiator may decide that one or more neutral experts should be retained to interpret the data and report to the parties. These neutral experts may be appraisers, accountants, doctors, lawyers, engineers, or other professionals. Their role is not adversarial. Procedures may be established for joint conversations with the neutral evaluator to test her approach and the accuracy of her findings.

Using Tactics or Power Plays

Tactics or power plays include everything from husband and wife playing "good cop, bad cop" in a car negotiation ("Well, I'd pay it, but my wife would kill me") to an insurance company subtly threatening to drag out litigation until the plaintiff runs out of money or energy to pursue the lawsuit. Good negotiators have thought through the potential tactics and have come up with ideas to try when they are used. Fortunately, there are numerous options, because an approach that works in one area will not necessarily work in another.

A few approaches include:

- Recognize the tactic. Once you know what the party is trying to do, you will have a better idea of how to respond.
- Identify the tactic out loud and then suggest a fair resolution. For example, if the other party is playing "good guy/bad guy" you may want to compliment them on their finesse and then suggest a fair standard by which to determine the price. This response reframes the

45

problem to an objective approach rather than a positional approach.

- Do not respond. Simply pause. Often it helps to ask a clarifying question and then pause until the other party has completely answered the question. This approach gives the other party the opportunity to explain his statement or position, and often lets him create his own trap. If you do not respond but make it apparent you are awaiting justification, he may continue talking to fill in uncomfortable spaces until he realizes that his tactic or position is unreasonable. In addition, pausing gives you time to calm down, think through the situation, and focus your energy on getting what you want rather than getting even with the other party.

- Where there truly is a difference in power (one party can fire the other; one party has vast resources; one party controls all of the witnesses, etc.), acknowledge the power difference, highlight the reasons it is in the party's best interest to find a solution, and work with him to find a resolution rather than fighting against him to "win" an unwinnable fight. This situation is one where it truly is important to understand your BATNA (*see* chapter 8) and be prepared to help the other side see how your actions affect him.

There are whole books on dealing with stumbling blocks and power issues in negotiation.[16] These ideas are just a few to highlight the possibilities and to show that what might appear to be insurmountable barriers may be overcome with patience, thought, and perseverance.

---

16. *Id.*; Ury, *supra* note 13; Karrass, *supra* note 12; Robert H. Mnookin, Andrew S. Tulumello, Scott Peppet, *Beyond Winning: Negotiating to Create Value in Deals and Disputes* (2000).

Attacks

For some reason, some negotiators think that they will gain an advantage by attacking the person with whom they are negotiating. If you recognize an attack as a tactic and refuse to take it personally, you can handle it effectively and gain ground. There are a number of ways to handle attacks and stonewalling:

- Ignore it and continue talking about the problem.

- Reframe the attack to make it productive:

  "I see you are concerned about meeting that deadline; how can we make sure everything is in place so the deadline can be met?"

  "I'm sorry if you think I am not negotiating in good faith. Let's discuss this issue more fully and see if we can't correct that perception."

  "I understand that there have been significant issues in the past. Let's work now on the issue that is before us and try to make this relationship work for the future."

  "That question looks only to my obligations. Let's talk about how we are going to make this contract work."[17]

- Address it head on in a calm and positive way. Then turn the conversation toward something productive. "I think I understand your concerns. Let's make sure that we keep them in mind as we continue. Now, let's talk about . . ."

---

17. Ury, *Getting Past No*, pp. 89–94.

Refusal to Move from Positions

- Ask questions that turn parties to look at their interests rather than their positions:

  "I understand your position. Let me understand how you got there."

  "Why do you need the deadline that you have set?"

  "What have you based that figure on?"

  "Why do you ask for this specific visitation schedule?"

  "How does our agreement on issue A play into your position here on issue B?"

- Then follow up with a discussion of the interests or needs expressed, ignoring the positions.

Especially when your opponent is aggressive and uncooperative, it is important to be aware of the tactics and to try a variety of your own. Chester Karrass says that the key to negotiating with an aggressive opponent is not to be predictable. Sometimes you should be aggressive, sometimes cooperative.[18] The key is to keep trying and to work to get the other party involved in the process of solving the problem at hand.

---

18. Karrass, *supra* note 12, at p. 131.

CHAPTER FIVE:
NEUTRAL EVALUATION

Neutral evaluation is an assessment of the likely trial outcome made by an attorney experienced in cases of the type at issue. The evaluation is made after the parties have had an opportunity to present the basic, core factual and legal contentions to the neutral. Although the process may build toward a mediation, technically, neutral evaluation is not a mediation. Indeed, mediation or other forms of ADR must wait until after the neutral either delivers the evaluation or at least has received the entire presentation by the parties. Thus, the process is not freewheeling like mediation. It requires an orderly presentation, opportunity for questions, and then the evaluation or an offer of discussions prior to delivery of the neutral's opinion. The process contemplates that the evaluator will not render the opinion in a piecemeal fashion. Instead, it is given in a relatively formal manner, often in writing.

The earlier a case can be disposed of by settlement, the lower the economic and psychological costs. In addition to these concerns of counsel and the client, the court too has an interest in clearing its dockets. The device of neutral evaluation is an ADR method that is finding favor among courts throughout the country. The plan is to get the case into an evaluative procedure from which a mediation or other settlement device can proceed promptly. Thus, in some courts, *early neutral evaluation*, or ENE, proceeds upon the filing of the answer. In most, however, a six-month period for discovery is permitted before the parties must commence neutral evaluation. Still, in other courts, where ADR devices are optional or where the parties may choose private ADR, the use of neutral evaluation comes later when the parties are well familiar with their case. In many instances, neutral evaluation is almost always followed by negotiation or mediation.

PURPOSE OF NEUTRAL EVALUATION

Lawyers and claims professionals are busy people. They tend to put off real analysis of their cases until they are forced into true preparation. One of the benefits of neutral evaluation is that it forces the participants to take a hard look at the case and prepare it for presentation. At bottom, the purpose of neutral evaluation really is to attack the sources of unnecessary cost and delay. It is designed to get past noncommunicative pleadings, find the center of the dispute, often without formal discovery and motion practice, overcome inertia, and focus the parties on the path to resolution.

In addition, a neutral evaluation may fulfill other functions. For example, it increases both client participation in and understanding of the process, while at the same time decreasing the intimidation of the client who may be frightened by the prospect of testifying in court. The process allows the clients to "have their day in court," both explaining their positions and, frequently, getting a chance to share their feelings or true reasons for bringing or defending the suit to the opposing party.

Perhaps most beneficial is the fact that the neutral's fresh perspective often helps clients or attorneys with unrealistic expectations gain a sense of reality, understanding, perhaps for the first time, that there is another side to the issue, with strong and perhaps convincing arguments to support it. Finally, the neutral's objectivity often helps her to offer creative, mutually beneficial settlement options. After hearing evidence and arguments presented by the parties and counsel, the neutral will give a frank evaluation of their positions and the value of the case, and provide an opportunity for discussion.

HOW IT WORKS

Once the neutral is selected either by the parties or appointed by the court, she meets with counsel to design the process. Typically, counsel will be asked to prepare and file an *evaluation statement*. This document is not given to the court. It contains the positions of the parties and is designed to prepare the neutral to hear the matter.

The initial meeting with the evaluator should also be utilized to determine who ought to be present at the evaluation. Certainly the client should attend together with such experts who may be necessary if their live presentation is desired. Usually, expert statements come in the form of reports rather than "testimony" at these meetings.

The parties and the neutral work to calendar the meeting, select a neutral location, and decide on just what should be presented. The neutral will make the process clear to counsel. She should discuss the issue of venting by parties and witnesses. She must also make it clear that this is not a mediation and that negotiation, if any, will not occur until all matters have been presented to her for evaluation.

At the session itself, the neutral will deliver an opening statement in which she will describe the process so that all participants will understand what follows. She should include the purposes of neutral evaluation in the statement. These, she will likely note, include reducing cost and delay, facilitating preparation by counsel on both fact and law issues, narrowing and defining issues, and moving the case either to resolution or preparation for trial. The neutral probably will point out her subject matter expertise in cases of this type.

The process she will describe permits plaintiff and defendant to make uninterrupted presentations of position and evidence. All questions will be held in abeyance until both presentations are completed. At the conclusion of the presentations, the evaluator will ask such questions as she thinks appropriate. The parties are then permitted to ask questions of each other. This is not writ in stone. The evaluator and the parties may create whatever orderly process that meets their needs.

After all the evidence is in, the evaluator may offer to permit the parties to negotiate by themselves or with her as mediator prior to rendering her evaluation. In the absence of a negotiating session, she will deliver an evaluation that comments, as appropriate, on the issues, evidence, and the likely jury verdict in the case. Evaluators are presenting an opinion not on the settlement value of the case but on the verdict.

Like the mediator, the evaluator has no power to resolve any issue or case. She is a facilitator of the discussion. By being in charge of the procedure, however, the neutral can test how realistic each party's evaluation of her case is, prepare a plan for information gathering—some of which can and should be a joint effort—and generally assist in aiming the case toward an early disposition. The more the parties are involved in discussions, the aim of which is settlement, the more likely that they will accept settlement rather than trial. All information provided to the neutral is considered confidential and is not admissible in court because it is a settlement negotiation.

The neutral evaluator brings to the process her experience trying, defending, hearing, or participating in similar cases in similar courts. In addition to whatever technical means the neutral uses to evaluate the case, the understanding of the process gained through years of experience will greatly influence the neutral's opinions. This experience brings a strong dose of reality to the evaluation process and helps the neutral explain the evaluation to the parties, often providing the first objective opinion of how a judge or jury in their particular case is likely to react. In addition to the innate understanding of the process, the neutral brings to the evaluation the technical tools necessary to analyze and derive a dollar figure verdict. This analysis is described more fully under the section on BATNA, in chapter 8.

CHAPTER SIX:
THE MEDIATION PROCESS

Mediation is, simply put, a facilitated negotiation. That means the parties work out the dispute themselves with the help of a neutral third party called a mediator. It sounds simple but it is really a complex process. Guiding people is much harder than telling them what to do. How to guide parties is a matter of personal style. But there is a set process and there are many techniques unique to mediation that will help you in finding the style and approach that works best for you and, for attorneys and clients, in finding the mediator that best suits their particular dispute. Mediation is designed to be the client's process. The clients are the ones best suited to discussing the issues and to figuring out the most workable resolution. For this reason, mediation is perfectly suited for almost any kind of dispute where an issue of law need not be interpreted in order for a resolution to be reached.

The mediator's job is to help the parties figure out how to resolve their dispute.[19] The mediator accomplishes this by using listening, communication, and negotiation skills. The resolution may be one that the mediator agrees with, or it may not. The real issues are whether the resolution is negotiated fairly and completely by the parties and whether the parties understand and accept their decision and its ramifications.

THE MEDIATOR'S ROLE

The key to mediating effectively is to understand that a mediator is in control of the process but not the outcome. By leaving

---

19. There are many who would argue that resolution is not the primary goal of mediation. Improving the relationship, exploring alternatives, providing the parties with the tools for future resolutions, as well as resolving this dispute, are all admirable goals of mediation.

the process to someone else, the parties and their lawyers can focus on the problem and its resolution. The process includes who speaks first, what topics are addressed in what order, how they are addressed, and when and how offers are conveyed.

Running the process starts with setting the tone and establishing ground rules. The mediator must build a relationship with the parties so they trust him and have confidence in his ability to help them. By setting a positive, professional tone, the mediator helps set expectations for how the parties will act. Basic ground rules will be set out at the beginning of the process, such as asking that parties not interrupt each other and when breaks will be taken.

Once a relationship is established and the parties are comfortable, the mediator will then guide the parties to begin the discussion of the problem. He will aid in the exchange of information while helping the parties manage their feelings and emotions about the problem. He must help the parties find ways to discuss options for resolution so they can solve their problem together and, finally, lead them to formulate an agreement or a plan for further negotiations. Each step is quite complex and requires the effective use of a variety of skills.

SKILLS OF AN EFFECTIVE MEDIATOR

Patience is perhaps the most important skill of a mediator. The mediator must understand that the problem before him is not his own problem and that parties reach resolution by a variety of paths and at different speeds. Having the patience to help the parties work through their emotions and to ensure that they have enough information to be prepared to resolve their dispute before diving into exploration of settlement options is essential.

Flexibility is also key. It is easy to listen to a discussion of a problem and jump to a conclusion as to how it should be resolved, or at least to see options for resolution. It rarely works that way. The parties have their own ideas (usually diametrically opposed), and their own needs that will affect how and what resolution is reached. They may explore one path of resolution for a while, and then change and resolve the dispute in a completely different way. It is not at all unusual for parties in an employment termination dispute to spend time discussing rehiring and all its related issues and then resolve it with a money settlement. A mediator must be flexible enough to guide each discussion, recognize when it is no longer productive, and switch gears while still making the parties feel that the process is productive and useful.

Good listening skills are essential. Chapter 4 discussed active listening and open-ended questions. The mediator has to be an expert in these areas. But there is an additional difficulty in mediation—not only does the person being listened to have to feel that the mediator cares and understands, but the mediator has to make sure that the *other* party both hears and understands what is being said while still feeling listened to and understood. One of the jobs of the mediator is to manage the communication between and among the parties. It is up to the mediator to manage and structure the discussions to move them along POSITIVE lines and to ensure ACCURACY. The mediator must also recognize when the party is posturing for his constituency rather than speaking for himself. The party also may attempt to support his own view by vague or actual allusions to what others believe about the problem. The neutral must assess what is said and try to move beyond the "public" face and on to the problem.

Neutrality is important. Not only does the mediator have to make everyone feel comfortable, then run the process, ask questions, and manage information, but he has to do it all while still making sure no one thinks he is biased. Maintaining neutrality involves ensuring that any opinions about what the parties "deserve" or who is "right" or "wrong" are not revealed. The mediator must make sure that he asks questions that do not come across as taking sides or agreeing with one party over the other.

THE MEDIATION PROCESS

Each mediation is unique and each mediator approaches dispute resolution differently. But there are basic parts to a mediation which are consistent. For example, each mediation begins before the parties meet. The mediator or case coordinator works with the parties and/or their attorneys to choose the best mediator, check for possible conflicts of interest, answer questions, and help the parties prepare for the mediation. Then, at the beginning of the mediation, the mediator does his *mediator's monologue*, where he explains the process and answers questions. After the monologue, the parties and their attorneys are each given an opportunity to make an *opening statement*, explaining the background, issues, and progress to date. After the openings, the mediator usually holds a *joint session*, where the parties discuss the preliminary issues and answer questions the mediator may have and, often, questions from the other parties. When joint session no longer seems productive, or it is clear that the parties need to speak with the mediator privately, the mediator calls a *caucus*. Caucus is a private meeting with one party or several parties and their attorneys, but not all the parties. This way, issues can be discussed openly which should not be discussed in front of the opposing party (*e.g.*, clarifying interests and priorities; exploring how realistic the party's assumptions are; formulating offers; deciding whether certain evidence should be revealed now or later, etc.).

In some mediations, the parties are able to work together, discussing important issues calmly and jointly considering options. Others may have many topics best discussed separately, in caucuses. Of course, each mediator is different, too. Individual styles have a profound effect on how the process is run. Some mediators are comfortable handling tension and anger, and keep the parties together as much as possible. Others prefer to encourage venting of emotions separately, and therefore conduct more caucuses. Each part of the mediation is discussed in detail below. All participants play important roles in each part and should understand both their role and the roles of the others involved in order to make the most of the process.

Pre-Mediation Discussions with Parties and Counsel

The first contact the mediator will have with the case usually is initiated by telephone from one of the parties, counsel, or an agent of a referring court or agency. It can be helpful for the mediator to talk to the parties and/or their lawyers prior to the actual commencement of the mediation. Many lawyers, and most clients, will have no clear idea of what the process is. A good deal of stress can be eliminated in conversations that explain what mediation is. It is best if the mediator, or in the case of a private provider, an experienced case coordinator, can hold a meeting with both sides. This will help establish rapport and promote trust in the mediator and the process. It also gives the mediator the opportunity to become familiar with the issues. If a conference is impractical, a telephone conference or separate telephone conversations will have to suffice. Often it is the case coordinator who holds this preliminary conference, discussing the practical aspects of mediation and answering the parties' questions.

Other significant benefits of a pre-mediation conference or call include the opportunity to:

- Explain the rules of confidentiality;

- Give each party the Agreement to Mediate (a copy of the RRC form is set out in appendix A);

- Determine who has the decision-making authority and advise the parties why the decision-maker must be present at the mediation;

- Discuss the need for documents or visits to relevant locations;

- Discuss the role of counsel at the mediation; and

- Calm the fears of a party unfamiliar with the process.

One of the issues the parties will face is determining what type of mediation they want and what skills or techniques they want the mediator to use. In a complex business dispute, for example, the parties may think it essential to have a mediator with sufficient business experience to understand the issues without the learning process so necessary for a jury. In a divorce mediation, the parties may want a mediator with a tax background, or perhaps a family counseling approach. They may feel that an aggressive, no-nonsense mediator is ideal, or that a soft-spoken, comforting and listening approach will be best. Those concerns should be thought through and discussed with opposing counsel, case coordinators, or mediators before someone is hired. References should be checked, as should conflicts of interest. It would be awkward to hire a mediator, only to find out the day of the mediation that the mediator is a major shareholder in the parent company whose financial security may be affected by the out-come of the dispute.

Types of Mediation

There are also several different styles of mediation. Mediation in its "purest" form is facilitative. As lawyers came into the process, it became more evaluative. And there is a group that thinks mediation should be transformative.

Facilitative Mediation

Historically, mediation began as a process to facilitate, or help, problem solving. The idea was to help people, who could not otherwise find a solution to their differences, find ways to resolve problems that did not require a third party making a decision. No jury, no judge, no arbitrator. The problem belongs to the parties and so must the solution. Therefore, facilitative mediators hold that mediators should not give their opinions (that's what lawyers, accountants, doctors, etc. are for), nor should they tell parties how to solve their dispute. In facilitative mediation, the mediator will ask rather than tell: "How will a jury come out on this issue?" "What will happen if you try a solution such as this one?" "What problems will you face if you take that position?"

Evaluative Mediation

Especially as lawyers and ex-judges became mediators, and as lawyers began to be in charge of setting up the mediation and choosing the mediator, an evaluative element has been added to facilitative mediation. Evaluative mediation is harder to define because there are so many variations. Some evaluative mediators are facilitative mediators who bring in evaluation if they feel the parties are completely stalled and will never move if the mediator does not provide an opinion ("I know you think this is a strong argument, but I've tried dozens of cases like this and juries never buy it because. . . ," or "I think you should try this approach because . . . ").

Others, often retired judges, give their opinion all the way through. They tell the parties what they think of the arguments and evidence presented, they often devise settlement options, or at the least they provide strong arguments supporting or rejecting options. These strongly evaluative mediators may be very effective with clients who simply cannot see reality—the client read the verdict in the McDonald's coffee case and thinks he, too, will get millions of dollars for his tragic situation. It is also helpful in a situation where both sides truly see the case from opposite viewpoints—each attorney believes a jury will evaluate the evidence in her party's favor. Often an experienced trial lawyer or retired judge can bring an objective perspective, differentiating cases and verdicts, discussing strengths and weaknesses, and helping the parties find a middle ground closer to the mediator's perceived realistic outcome.

Good evaluative mediators provide opinions only when requested or after being given permission by all parties. Most opinions are voiced in caucus, *infra*, so that parties do not lose face in front of each other and are better able to ask questions and assess the information being provided. And effective evaluative mediators do not use their expertise to tell the parties what to do; they use it to help the parties have a realistic basis upon which to form a resolution.

Transformative Mediation

There is a movement to use mediation for purposes greater than simply dispute resolution. Robert A. Baruch Bush and Joseph Folger believe that mediation can be used to engender moral growth.[20] Some large companies have adopted the philosophy that talk, when facilitated by well-trained mediators, can help people move beyond their disputes. At the same time, proponents of transformative mediation expect mediation to help the parties develop better understanding with and empathy toward each other. They believe that teaching the parties how to communicate better and to work together enables them to resolve their disputes.

This approach involves teaching parties communication skills, negotiation techniques, and listening. While these goals are admired by all, there is significant hesitation about mediation's ability to make such vast changes. Most mediators are of the opinion that transformation does occur in some mediations and that helping people grow to understand the opinions and needs of others can be a useful part of mediation, but that mediation is designed primarily as a tool for helping people resolve their disputes. Any transformation achieved is a pleasant by-product of dispute resolution. "Every good mediator takes advantage of transformative moments."[21]

AGREEMENT TO MEDIATE

Each mediator or mediation organization has its own form of Agreement to Mediate, which the parties execute prior to the opening of the actual mediation. *See* the Resolution Resources Corporation (RRC) form contract reprinted in appendix A. Note that the agreement explains a number of important matters that the mediator will reiterate in his opening monologue at the start of the proceeding. These include:

- Getting the parties to affirm their intention to work to settle the case;

---

20. Robert A. Baruch Bush and Joseph P. Folger, *The Promise of Mediation: Responding to Conflict through Empowerment and Recognition* (Jossey-Bass 1994).

21. Betty Manley, nationally recognized mediator and trainer.

- The requirement of disclosure of information necessary to the resolution of the dispute;

- Confidentiality and exceptions to the rule;

- That the mediator does not offer legal or other professional advice to the parties;

- Encouragement to retain counsel and to involve them in mediation; and

- Termination of the process.

BEGINNING THE MEDIATION SESSION

As the mediation begins, the mediator will set up the room so that it is comfortable, and then arrange the parties and attorneys to minimize tension and maximize productive interaction. Usually this means placing the parties on opposite sides of the table with the parties closest to the mediator. The mediator will then try to establish a positive tone for the meeting so the parties can learn to trust him and feel that this process will be successful. Some mediators accomplish these goals through friendly conversation, others through businesslike efficiency. Some take just a moment or two; others spend as much time as they feel necessary. A simple discussion of last night's game can be enough to ease the tension and start people talking to each other. Then the mediator will go on to the *mediator's monologue* and introduce the process.

THE MEDIATOR'S MONOLOGUE

The purpose of the monologue is to continue establishing rapport with the parties and to make sure everyone understands the process. Usually it is helpful to bring a checklist to make sure you do not leave anything important out of the monologue. Even experienced mediators continue to bring their checklist. A sample opening statement checklist is attached at appendix B.

It is important to make sure the parties know your name and what you wish to be called. A tone of either formality or informality is fine, but it needs to be established early so the parties are comfortable. It is also important that the mediator know the parties' names and roles so that he can speak comfortably and keep the parties involved.

The Agreement to Mediate should be reviewed and signed, and the important concepts contained within it should be discussed. Having the parties understand the obligations of confidentiality and its exceptions is essential. Generally, the agreement provides that anything said or revealed during the mediation will be held confidential from anyone not present during the mediation. In addition, the mediator must explain that anything stated in private caucus will be held confidential from those not in the caucus unless the parties give permission to reveal it. The parties should understand that there are exceptions to these obligations, too. For example, if a party reports an intention to commit a crime or to harm someone, the mediator has an obligation to reveal that information to the proper authorities. The parties must also know that the process is voluntary and that they are not required to take any steps that could be construed as an agreement to resolve the dispute. Understanding that the mediator is not acting in any professional capacity (lawyer, financial advisor, psychologist) other than as neutral facilitator is also essential.

Then the mediator must clarify the process. Even parties who have had the process explained by their attorney rarely understand it until they are sitting in the room. And those who have participated in mediations before need to know how this particular mediator runs the process—does he concentrate on joint sessions? Does he talk mostly to the attorneys or encourage participation by the parties? Does he require that the parties specify what information will be kept confidential from each caucus or does he hold everything confidential unless given permission to reveal it? (*See* further discussion below).

Finally, the mediator should answer any questions and get a joint commitment to begin (anything from "Are we ready to start?" to "Does everybody feel they are ready to make a commitment to this process?").

It is helpful at the end of the monologue if the mediator explains what he wants the parties to discuss in the opening statement.

Who should talk? What should they cover? How does this opening statement differ from the one they would make in court? Also, it is useful to repeat the ground rule that each party allow the other to finish his statement without interruption.

PARTIES' OPENING STATEMENTS

Because the mediation process is different from litigation, opening statements are also different. Often the opening statement is the first opportunity the client has to speak his piece—what happened, how it affected him, the problems caused, and how he feels about it. It is also often the first time opposing counsel will see what a great witness this party will make at trial. Parties should be well prepared to maximize this opportunity, both so that they can say what they need to say to be prepared to move to resolution, and to maximize their settlement potential in the eyes of the other parties. The attorney's ideal role is to discuss the procedural issues (where the dispute is in the legal process, prior settlement negotiations, issues that remain outstanding, etc.) and the legal issues.

Everyone should keep in mind, however, that this opportunity is an excellent one for setting a positive tone and making sure the opposing parties know that settlement or resolution is the goal. Opening statements that point fingers, establish fixed positions, or are condescending merely decrease the chance of resolution. Parties can explain how much pain they are in, how dramatically their lives have been affected, how hurt they were by the others' actions, all in great detail, without causing the other party to get defensive or, worse, walk out. (*See* communication, chapter 4, and specifically discussion on *I statements*.)

The mediator also has an important role during and after the parties' opening statements. He must:

- Listen closely to hear the parties discuss issues, interests, and needs;
- Understand the concerns raised by each party;
- Help the parties really hear each other by clarifying, reframing, or otherwise restating the important points made in each opening;

- Recognize common interests and issues; and
- Start creating an agenda by which to guide the parties through the issues.

JOINT SESSIONS

After the opening statements, there is much variation in how mediators conduct the process. Some go immediately into caucus. Others use a brief joint session and then break into caucus, while still others use joint session unless they absolutely must go into caucus, and even then, use caucus briefly and sparingly. Perhaps the best mediators vary their methods depending upon the type of dispute, the needs of the parties, and the issues raised.

The purpose of holding a joint session, or sessions, is to encourage the parties to understand and exchange information, to work on their relationship, or to continue a productive dialogue. These sessions are particularly important if the parties have a relationship that will continue beyond the end of the dispute. For example, divorcing parents will have to continue to work together to raise their children; if it is possible to help them begin forging a relationship that is separate and yet recognizes mutual interests and needs, joint sessions may be essential.

The issues mediators will face in joint session include:

- How much information should be exchanged jointly and how to encourage the exchange;
- How high to allow emotions to escalate before separating parties;
- How to diffuse emotions and turn parties toward problem solving; and
- When to break off a joint session.

Unfortunately, there are no bright line rules to answer any of these issues. The mediator must keep in mind, however, that anything destructive should be stopped before it destroys or harms the process. So, while it may be essential that the parties work through their emotions, it may be better to let the emotional party vent in caucus, or to use a caucus to guide him on how to vent productively in joint session.

One complaint about inexperienced mediators is that they break into caucus too soon. By using communication skills, taking charge of the process, and providing guidance, joint sessions can be extremely helpful even in hotly contested disputes. For example, where parties are unable to talk together on some issues, a mediator may use a caucus to teach the parties how to use *I statements* or to practice techniques for communicating controversial information before even beginning the joint discussion of issues that are the basis for the mediation. This way, the parties will see that they are able to work together, and will become invested in the process and, thus, more likely to keep working toward a complete resolution.

CAUCUS

A caucus is a private meeting between the mediator and one party—or several but not all parties—to explore new options, to clarify proposals, to allow the parties to cool down, to gather facts for the mediator's use, or to give the parties a break from negotiations. It also allows the non-caucusing party to meet with his own party members, to make necessary phone calls, and to rest. Either the mediator or one of the parties may request a caucus.

When to Caucus

Caucus may be used whenever the mediator thinks it will be useful. Caucusing at different times throughout the process may accomplish different goals.

Early in the process:

- Allows parties to vent anger and hostility;
- Allows setting of guidelines for expression of emotions during joint sessions;
- Answers any questions about the process and the roles of the parties and the mediator, and establishes guidelines for behavior, procedure, and communications;
- Establishes rapport between the mediator and each party;

- Helps parties identify and clarify issues; and
- Discovers actual positions or leads to realistic interests and needs, which may be different from those stated in the opening statement or joint session.

In the midst of negotiation:

- Focuses on preventing premature commitment to a position;
- Clarifies issues or relevant facts, and corrects misperceptions about parties, facts, or issues;
- Discusses forms of proposals and better ways to communicate ideas and concerns in joint sessions;
- Generates potential alternatives;
- Discusses bargaining power or ability;
- Begins to generate proposals for settlement;
- Allows parties to step back and consider negotiations without the pressure of the other party's presence; and
- Allows discussion of consequences of dragging out procedure or of hurrying settlement.

Near end of negotiations:

- Discusses settlement proposals based on information and issues known only to party and mediator;
- Develops settlement options;
- Discusses methods for implementation of proposed settlement;
- Breaks deadlocks; and
- Discusses and overcomes psychological pressures against settlement.

How to Caucus

- Choose a location separate enough for private, candid discussions.
- Decide with whom to caucus first. Early in negotiations it might be the initiator of the lawsuit or mediation.

Later it might be the most inflexible party or the one whose emotions might become intrusive in the negotiations; be sure to caucus with all parties.

- Be supportive of each party in caucus without taking sides. Empathize with them; understand their interests and options. Be careful of mixed messages, however. Empathy may come across as agreement with one party over the other.

- Be firm—in private you can help the parties explore the reality of a proposal or position. If you feel the party is being unreasonable or is taking an unworkable hard-line approach, work it through in the caucus. This way no one loses face.

- Help parties devise options or propose hypothetical options, and work through them so the party understands underlying misgivings and the effect on his interests. Make sure the party feels that the proposal made to the other party is his own, not the mediator's idea.

- Clarify which information the party wishes to keep confidential. If sharing some information might lead to a more acceptable solution, discuss whether this information should be shared.

The confidentiality of the caucus session often can be essential to the success of the mediation.[22] The parties must understand that everything said during the caucus will be kept confidential from everyone not in that caucus unless they give permission for

---

22. There is significant controversy over how important the assurance of confidentiality is both in caucus and in the mediation process itself. *See* Reporter's Working Notes, Uniform Mediation Act (Draft) §§ 5–8, National Conference of Commissioners on Uniform State Laws (Feb. 2001).

the mediator to reveal it.[23] Confidentiality is essential in caucus; the parties can reveal their true interests, hidden agendas, or needs they want met without discussing them publicly in joint session. The confidentiality of the caucus also allows the mediator and the parties to discuss openly and honestly the weaknesses and problems with their position or case.

There are state laws and often ethical decisions from the state bar or courts regarding confidentiality. These parameters should be stated and discussed before caucusing.

SETTING THE AGENDA

After the opening statements of the parties have been concluded, it is wise for the mediator to make certain that he understands the primary issues. He should state his own understanding of the issues that the parties wish to discuss, placing them in an orderly agenda. Usually, issues on which the parties have little or no disagreement should be handled first. Finding common ground and reaching agreement, even on small matters, sets a good psychological tone for the more difficult items that lie ahead.

Establishing a Positive Emotional Climate

In addition to facilitating communication, the mediator often must create an emotional climate conducive to clear communication and joint problem solving. Mediators use a variety of techniques to promote a positive emotional climate:

- Preventing interruptions or verbal attacks;

---

23. Some mediators prefer to inform the parties that the only things that will be kept confidential from the caucus are those things the party informs the mediator he wants kept confidential. The issue for the mediator is deciding whom he wants to have the burden for determining what should be confidential. The key for the parties is that they understand the rule and can rely on its consistent application.

- Encouraging parties to focus on the problem and not each other;

- Translating value-laden or judgmental language of disputants into less emotionally charged terms;

- Affirming clear descriptions or statements, procedural suggestions, or gestures of good faith while not taking sides on substantive issues;

- Accepting the expression of feelings and being empathetic while not taking sides;

- Reminding parties about behavioral guidelines that they have established;

- Diffusing threats by restating specific threats in terms of general pressure to change; and

- Intervening to prevent conflict escalation.

JOINT PROBLEM SOLVING

While maintaining the smooth running of the process, the mediator must figure out how to help the parties solve their problem. Here, of course, is the greatest challenge. And this is where mediation becomes an art that is aided by the application of a variety of skills. Communication skills, as discussed in detail in chapter 4, are absolutely essential. The when, where, and how much is the art. *Reality testing* techniques are also important. The ability to help parties understand and confront reality without becoming defensive is difficult to say the least. Helping parties balance power issues, set priorities, find common interests, and negotiate effectively is all part of joint problem solving.

FINDING COMMON INTERESTS

Common interests form the basis for one party to understand the other party in an effort to reach a mutually acceptable agreement. Each party has his own interests and the mediator must help the other party see that those interests are valid and must be considered throughout the process. Yet many of those interests will not coincide and may be contradictory.

In order to begin joint discussions leading to a resolution, the mediator must help the parties search for common interests. The mediator might start by discussing these interests and helping the parties understand which interests they have in common. For example, divorcing parents generally share the interest of finding a visitation schedule that works best for the children. Even in a personal injury case, the parties share the common interests of getting the dispute behind them and minimizing costs to reach resolution. Understanding how much they have in common often helps parties realize that a mutually acceptable solution really is possible. To help find common interests, mediators often:

- Use active listening skills as the parties discuss their views of the conflict;

- Reframe statements in an attempt to keep the parties discussing interests rather than positions;

- Directly question the parties as to their interests (this process may be difficult if the parties refuse to move away from positional bargaining or are trying to hide their interests and motives.);

- Ask the parties to discuss the situation while focusing on the interests or elements they feel necessary to a satisfactory solution;

- Brainstorm, either jointly or in caucus, on all of the interests affected by the situation;

- Determine which issues need to be resolved before others can be explored, and determine which issues are related and must be discussed simultaneously; and

- Explore perceptions of interests. Parties may perceive their interests to be at odds with the interests of the other party, or they may perceive the other party's interests incorrectly. The mediator will help the parties understand everyone's interests and the priority of issues as they relate to these interests.

Finally, to further the process, the mediator may discuss the overlap in interests and needs in order to narrow the differences between the parties.

REALITY TESTING

Helping parties understand the reality of their situation and its possible solutions is one of the main reasons attorneys suggest mediation to their clients. For every plaintiff who wins a multi-million dollar verdict against a major chain for hot coffee, there are probably fifty whose equally valid cases were dismissed. Attorneys are paid to give realistic advice, but also to be the strongest advocate for the client. It is difficult to balance reality testing with advocating. Good mediators are able to help the attorneys find that balance without telling them what to do and how to do it.

Some of the key points of reality testing are:

- It is almost always done in caucus. Parties become very defensive when confronted in front of their opponent with questions like "What is the demand for $500,000 based upon?" or "What evidence do you have to support this argument?"

- It is used only after the parties are ready to hear it. Pushing parties to face reality is difficult; doing it when they are still too emotional to listen and to react reasonably is pointless.

- Reality should never be thrown at the parties—a party is likely to walk out of the room if the mediator, right after openings, says "You can't win this case; the most you can do is get enough to cover your expenses." But later, after exploring and understanding needs, interests, and evidence, a mediator can ask lots of questions which lead the party to the same conclusion—"If you tried this case ten times, how many times would you win?" "What is a likely recovery?" "What's the most likely scenario?" "What do the jury summaries show is likely to happen?" "Why do you think your opponent is so convinced he is going to win and not have to pay anything?"

Often it is helpful for the mediator to think about potential reality testing questions before beginning a mediation. If you know it is a case involving employment discrimination allegations, possible questions for the employee include:

- What evidence do you have?
- How will the company counter your evidence?
- What will your witnesses say?
- What have juries done in similar cases?
- How has this company fared in similar lawsuits?
- In similar cases where juries have found discrimination, what have the damages been?
- Why do you think the employer is making that offer?
- What really is your priority here? (Keeping the job, ending the discrimination, monetary damages)
- What will happen if you do not reach agreement here today?

One of the hardest things about reality testing is knowing when to stop and when to keep pushing. Clients and their attorneys rarely admit their true weaknesses without any pushing. A strong mediator can use questions effectively to steer parties to better understand the other party's side, how realistic their own demands are, and where realistic settlement options lie. Offers and demands should not be made before the mediator has conducted at least some reality testing to better understand the parties' needs and interests. "How important is this point to you?" "Why do you think the other party feels so strongly about that point?" "Where is the overlap of interests here?"

Then, when helping the parties come up with their offers and demands, the mediator can use these realities to help them create workable solutions. "How can this offer meet their need for stability?" "Given your priority of getting the settlement money soon and their stated need to minimize costs, what demand can you make so they can meet your time schedule?"

And in helping parties evaluate the offers or demands of the other party, reality testing is essential. "Why do you think they made this demand?" "In what ways does this offer meet your needs?" "How can we work with the acceptable parts of their offer to create a realistic and significant move toward resolution?" "If I take this offer to them, what should I say when they object that it does not appear to be a good faith move toward settlement?" Pushing the parties to address these issues not only makes the mediator's job easier, it makes the parties stop and consider the effect of their actions. A mediator who simply takes offers back and forth without reality testing at each step is not providing any real service.

Reality testing is one of the places where evaluative and facilitative mediation differ. Facilitative mediators would say, "You (attorney) have tried similar cases before this judge. Have any of them ever allowed this kind of motion?" Evaluative mediators might say something like, "You know a court will never allow this motion." Each technique is effective in the right context with certain types of clients and attorneys. A good evaluative mediator will use facilitative techniques first, and only become evaluative if it becomes apparent the client simply is not understanding or is more likely to accept the same information from the mediator than from his own attorney.

THE AGREEMENT

When the parties have exchanged enough information and vented enough emotion to turn to solving the problem at hand, the next problem is helping the parties generate options and offers. An important point that is overlooked by many mediators and by attorneys is that people need to feel that they had an important role in reaching the agreement. They need to think it was their idea. If a mediator or a lawyer tells the client what the best solution is, the client will respond with resistance. Often in mediation a new mediator will "know" the best solution very early. While that solution may in fact be the ideal solution, if it is suggested by the mediator too early, it will be resisted and may even set the parties back into their positional roles.

It is important, then, that the option generation procedures be followed and the mediator and attorneys limit their role to helping the parties come up with solutions and analyze them. Of course, it is the attorney's job to advise her client on whether an option is a good one, to point out the problems, and to help the client examine how each option meets the client's needs and interests. There are times when parties are unable or unwilling to develop options. At that point, it is possible for attorneys and mediators to make suggestions, mostly from the point of "Would it work if you did something like *this*...?" rather than "I think you should do *this* for these reasons."

PROBLEM SOLVING

There are a number of approaches to helping the parties turn to problem solving.

First, generate settlement options:

- Work on the simplest problems first. Once you have some agreement, the parties will be more likely to continue negotiating.

- Consider whether a package solution will be necessary, taking into account all of the interests simultaneously rather than dealing with some issues separately.

- Brainstorm, either jointly or in caucus, about all possible options without judging any of them.

- The mediator might suggest some options that have worked in previous situations and allow the parties to work with the suggestions to refine them to work in their situation.

Next, evaluate the options:

- Caucus may be helpful with considering options in light of all stated interests and confidential information.

- If the parties work well together, allow the discussion to continue to establish objective criteria for evaluating options.

- Discuss and minimize unrealistic requests or positions.

- Discard unrealistic or unacceptable options.

- Emphasize interests and steer away from positional bargaining.

- Consider whether each option meets all parties' substantive needs, both in the short and long term.
- Consider the effect of each option on the relationship of the parties.
- Discuss potential problems with implementation of any proposed option.

Then, begin to formulate proposals:

- Usually this step is done in caucus.
- Consider whether an offer should be general or specific, contingent or not.
- Evaluate each offer in light of everyone's interests and identify how it will benefit all the parties.
- Evaluate risks involved in making each offer and whether the other party can be convinced to take similar risks.
- Consider whether the offer should be oral or written and, if written, who should write it. Sometimes it makes sense for the mediator to write a proposal and then allow the parties to comment on the draft until it becomes a document, written or shaped by the parties and therefore easier to accept. Usually the terms of the agreement should be written by the parties or a subgroup of the parties with the help of the mediator.

Finally, meet to discuss the proposal(s):

- Discuss how the proposal meets the substantive and emotional interests of all parties. Make sure specific tangible exchanges result from the proposal.
- Refine the proposal to take into account any interests not considered, problems with implementation, or other concerns raised.
- Make sure the proposal is mutually beneficial and, if possible, the best alternative available to the parties. Consider whether better options, such as trial or arbitration, exist. Try not to let the parties accept the proposal prematurely.

- Evaluate whether the proposal is comprehensive enough to resolve all of the issues in the dispute.

- Determine whether the resolution is final and permanent and whether the long term effect is as acceptable as the short term effect.

- Decide whether the solution will create an acceptable precedent for the parties to work from in resolving future conflicts.

- Discuss whether the proposal will really work to meet everyone's needs and interests.

REACHING AGREEMENT

In preparing, analyzing, and drafting agreements, you must consider the degree of settlement of all issues that is necessary and desirable for each situation. In a situation where the parties have to work together, a non-self-executing agreement, one that requires continuing performances or exchanges over a period of time, may be the best solution. In this way, the parties are free to continue working together to achieve the best solution as unexpected conditions occur. On the other hand, in a union situation or where the parties want a one-time solution, a self-executing agreement often works best. A self-executing agreement is one that settles all issues immediately and usually involves some tangible exchange, such as goods or services. No continuing involvement is necessary.

To create a strong agreement that will leave little to interpretation:

- Write it down.

- Provide for substantive exchanges—money, goods, services, apologies.

- Be comprehensive. Consider and provide for all possible contingencies.

- Make it clear that the agreement is a final resolution and add a waiver of all past disputes or at least all past related disputes.

- Do not provide for continuing or future performances that could raise questions or require interpretation.

- Set out consequences for failure to abide by the agreement. Preferably make the consequences enforceable without help from a court or third party.

- Make sure that the clauses are clear and leave nothing or little to interpretation.

- Where necessary, provide such detailed provisions that leave the parties no room to maneuver around the agreement.

- Make sure all legal issues are considered and that the agreement meets all legal requirements (the attorneys should take a large role in this part).

If the attorney for one of the parties is going to do the actual drafting of the final agreement, you may want to direct the parties' discussion to a general outline of all necessary provisions and jot them down in a *memo of understanding* or in an outline for the attorney's future use.

WHO SHOULD DRAFT THE AGREEMENT?

After all of the terms are agreed upon, the parties must decide how to write up their agreement and who should be responsible for the writing. Each option has advantages and disadvantages.

- One of the parties may draft the agreement in a caucus and all the parties may revise it in joint session. This option will work where the parties are able to work well together and where they trust the drafting party to write a fair proposal.

- The parties may draft the agreement jointly. Often this approach leads to haggling over details, but if it is successful, it leads to "buy in" by all the parties.

- A subcommittee of representatives from each party may draft the agreement, either in separate meetings or after the negotiations are through. This approach saves time for some of the party members and allows the details to be ironed out in a smaller group. This approach may be time-consuming in that the larger group will have to be consulted and their concerns taken into account at some point.

- The mediator may draft the agreement—often with the help of the parties. This way, the terms will not be subject to interpretation and possible misunderstanding. There will be little chance of bias, and the language used may be positive and nonjudgmental. Any details that were not discussed previously can be ironed out during this process.

- The attorneys may draft the agreement. This way, all legal issues will be addressed. The spirit of the agreement and the positive tone may be altered. This method avoids the problem of having lawyers alter agreements after the parties feel they have reached a final draft. Usually, in disputes when lawyers are involved, the final agreement will and should be drafted by the attorneys.

CHAPTER SEVEN:
SPECIAL PROBLEMS THAT ARISE DURING MEDIATION

Any number of things can delay resolution or get in the way of it. Communication skills and patience will help mediators handle most situations. There are certain situations, however, that arise often enough or pose sufficient problems to warrant more in-depth discussion.

SPECIFIC PROBLEMS

LYING OR GIVING FALSE INFORMATION

If a mediator suspects a lie, he should ask clarifying questions to reveal the truth. One way to keep the parties talking is to pretend not to understand what was said and to keep digging until the fallacies are corrected or revealed.

If a lie is discovered during a caucus, the mediator has several options.

- Suggest an independent expert to provide accurate information, where appropriate.

- Withdraw from the negotiations. Consider what to tell the other party about the withdrawal given confidentiality obligations.

- Confront the party and refuse to continue on the basis of the lie. Explain that mediation can only work if the parties are truthful and above-board with each other. Try to convince the party that the lie will come back to haunt him in the future.

- The mediator may have to consider going to the authorities with the information. If an illegal scheme or threats of harm to persons become apparent, the mediator must consider the consequences of failure to report. (*See* the ethics rules in appendix C and chapter 11.)

BAD SETTLEMENTS

Bad settlements may occur when parties are talked into agreements that are not in their best interest or that clearly are more favorable to the other party. The mediator cannot stop the parties from entering into such agreements. He can, however, ensure that the parties see the inequities of the agreement before allowing the agreement to be drafted or signed. A mediator may choose not to be a party to the agreement if he is concerned about its fairness. *See* the discussion of self-determination and agreements in chapter 11.

The best settlements are those that consider all of the interests and options in a realistic manner and can be implemented without further interference or conflict. As the parties near an agreement, the mediator should determine whether the agreement will meet these goals. If the settlement involves deception or bad faith on the part of one or more parties, the mediator must consider his actions.

- If a mediator knows that a settlement will be illegal or will entail illegal actions, he must either refuse to be a part of the settlement, advise the parties that they should get legal advice as to the legality of the settlement, or report the parties to the proper authorities. Ethical obligations are discussed more fully in chapter 11.

- The mediator should help the parties understand if their settlement will have an adverse effect on nonparties. If so, they should reconsider in light of potential future litigation, bad feelings, or publicity.

Remember, a mediator is not acting as an attorney or as an accountant or whatever his specialty may be. The mediator is chosen in part because of his specialty, and that knowledge should be used in managing the negotiations. The mediator is not there to provide legal or accounting advice. If the mediator feels that such advice is needed, he should suggest bringing in an expert as a co-mediator to provide independent evaluations. If he feels that there may be enforceability problems with an agreement, he should suggest that the parties consult their attorneys.

LAST MINUTE CLINKERS

You think you have a deal. Then someone raises an issue she forgot to mention. Or suddenly you find that the person, who said she had authority to settle, needs to check with her boss. How do you handle the situation so the whole deal does not fall through?

LAST MINUTE DEMANDS

- If one party makes a last-minute demand, suggest that the issue be dealt with in a separate mediation session. Offer to set up the time and place right then so he will understand that you are not trying to brush him off.

- Take a break. Everyone will be able to calm down, consider the demand, and attempt a response.

- If the demand is clearly a power play, identify it as such in a caucus. Then work with the parties to eliminate it or to handle it so that the problem is fully resolved.

LACK OF AUTHORITY

- When one party suddenly states that he does not have authority to settle, ask what his authority is. Ask who has the necessary authority and suggest that you talk directly to that person rather than waiting for the party to blame suggested changes on his "hard-hearted partner." Remind him of the contract he signed in which he represented that he had full authority.

- Suggest that you treat the proposed agreement as a draft and allow all parties to reconsider or present it to higher-ups. If both parties are allowed to make changes, the equivocating party may be more likely to agree.

UNWILLINGNESS TO AGREE

- If one party suddenly becomes unwilling to sign an agreement or to finalize the agreement, take the time to find out why.

- A caucus may be necessary to see whether confidential concerns are not being addressed by the agreement.

- Determine whether the party feels that he participated fully and explored all options. Sometimes allowing the party to make minor changes will ensure that he is now committed to the agreement as his own.

- Where necessary, suggest options for minor modifications to the agreement.

- Devise a method by which the party can save face and make his concerns known.

- Go through the arithmetic of considering the party's BATNA and WATNA (discussed in more detail in chapter 11) with them. If the consideration leads to a better alternative, your negotiations may be over. Or they may be just beginning.

DISAGREEMENTS BETWEEN CLIENTS AND COUNSEL

Understanding that the client holds the ultimate power to settle the dispute is important. Occasionally, counsel will tell a mediator that she wants her client to participate in a mediation because it is believed that the party has an unrealistic evaluation of the case. The use of a neutral evaluator can help in this situation.

The mediator who learns in the middle of the proceeding that the party and his attorney are very far apart in their estimates of the case may be in for trouble. Sometimes counsel and the client are unable to agree on the amount and nature of their own offer to the other side. The neutral can find himself in the position of trying to mediate between counsel and client. The mediator may attempt to use reality checks in the hopes of moving the "side" toward a unity of position. If the disagreement is fundamental, however, the effort will be unsuccessful and frustrating. Thus, if, for example, the party is really seeking vindication of his rights while counsel is trying to force her client into a settlement, the proper role of the mediator is to encourage a private caucus between the party and the attorney in the hope that they can find a common position.

POWER PLAYS

POWER OF THE PARTIES

The parties to a conflict have power both over each other and over the mediator. The mediator must be aware of the means of power and of the methods by which the parties use their power in order to manage the mediation effectively. For example, the parties will attempt to manipulate the mediator into supporting their positions. Some lawyers representing their clients will "try" the case to the mediator. The mediator must be careful not to nod too vigorously as if he agrees with the party's statements. He must also be careful not to make statements suggesting that he thinks one party is right and the other is wrong. At all times he must maintain his impartiality. Without impartiality, the mediator loses credibility. This can be a particular difficulty in the caucus. In caucus, there is a free exchange of views that can create the impression that the mediator is on the party's side or has taken sides with the other party.

Another tactic that the mediator should be aware of is the forming of coalitions between parties (especially in a large multiparty conflict). By combining power, the parties will have more influence over the outcome. If possible, the mediator must continually reiterate the importance of joint problem solving rather than coalition building. Some of these problems can be avoided with the use of co-mediators.

In addition, the mediator must understand the power of the parties over each other. There may be monetary ties, working relationships, or other ways in which the parties will continue to influence each other. For example, in a divorce case, the parties will have long-term influence over the way the children are raised, and the interaction of the former couple must continue as long as custody is shared. Concerns about power must be addressed, if not directly, then through the solution reached.

POWER OF THE MEDIATOR

The mediator may be seen as having the power to make the negotiations successful or a waste of time. Obviously, the real power for success or failure rests with the parties, but a mediator has a profound effect on how the final outcome is determined. Methods of influence must be flexible to meet the needs and styles of the parties in each instance. Most importantly, the mediator has the responsibility to set the tone for the negotiations and the duty to maintain a positive tone and a cooperative atmosphere throughout.

To set a positive tone:

Planning is essential

- Plan your opening, and carefully consider timing for and order of opening statements of the parties.

- Carefully consider an appropriate agenda; be prepared to alter it after hearing the opening statements of the parties. Make sure the parties understand and agree with your agenda or come up with a workable agenda of their own.

- Gain an understanding of the issues and the interests involved.

- Find common ground.

- Resolve a simple issue. This tactic will give the parties confidence that the process is working.

Use power to keep the parties on an equal plane

- Empower parties with no power.

- Keep access to information equal.

- Intercede to prevent intimidation.

Empowering parties with no apparent power can be accomplished in a number of ways. First, reality testing is essential to help the party with the power understand what power the other party really does have. For example, even an at-will employee has the power to affect the attitudes of coworkers, slowing down work as the employees discuss and take sides on the ongoing struggle. Next, the unempowered party needs to see what power he does have—the power to help the company rewrite a policy that affects all employees; the power to keep an insurance company in litigation until the dispute is actually resolved; the power to affect the reputation of a company by taking it to court or talking to the media.

Keeping access to information equal is especially difficult where attorneys are involved. Counsel understandably may resist production of material if the matter is in active litigation or likely to be so. If the material would be discoverable in the ordinary course of a lawsuit, it will not be difficult for the mediator to obtain disclosure. The problem lies where the material would not be discoverable, say because of privilege. No attorney wants to be in the position of having waived an evidentiary privilege. If the material is at the heart of the dispute, the mediator can help the parties decide how much they are willing to risk for a settlement. Counsel may enter into a formal agreement stipulating that the exchange of information for the purpose of this mediation will not be raised by either party as a waiver of a privilege in any subsequent or existing litigation. The agreement will hold for these parties. It cannot bind nonparties to these proceedings. Thus, some risk attends this type of disclosure, but counsel will likely be aware of the degree of risk in her particular case.

Of course, intimidation tactics are an old lawyer (and businessperson) standby. Fortunately, many participants are reluctant in mediation to use a tactic so clearly contrary to the goal of mediation. For those who refuse to leave their tactics out of the mediation, strong reality testing in caucus usually makes a difference. Also, understanding that the other party will not stand for it, that any physical intimidation will be reported immediately, and that the person is doing far more harm than good may go a long way toward helping the intimidating party find a more reasonable approach.

WALKOUTS

What do you do when a party threatens to walk out or actually walks out?

BEFORE THE PARTY LEAVES

Try to talk to the party before he leaves the premises. Talk about his unwillingness to negotiate. Is he still unsure of the process? Has he not become sufficiently involved to have a stake in the process? Is he trying to gain a concession up front simply because he has agreed to negotiate? Does he think he cannot gain through mediation? Does he think he will lose face by negotiating? In other words, determine why he is leaving and seek to talk him back into the room.

DISCUSS YOUR OPTIONS

To convince the party to return at this time:

- Suggest that the negotiations be conducted through his lawyer or other third-party go-betweens.

- Consider whether written communication only may be sufficient.

- Discuss the impact of his refusal to negotiate. He may not understand the costs of litigation or the risks of allowing the situation to escalate or drag on. Try to get him to see that he would expect the other party to behave differently and he would not want nonparties to get the impression that he is unwilling to negotiate on anything.

If he has already left:

- Discuss with the other party whether he wants to try again. If so, call or write the party or his attorney if you think it would be more beneficial.

- Discuss the reasons for the walkout. Determine whether the problems can be overcome in a second session.

- Suggest alternatives for avoiding the same problems. Perhaps a different representative for one or both parties should be present. Perhaps more private caucuses are necessary. If preferable, the mediation could be conducted over the telephone with only the mediator and one party making contact at a time.

- Set up a time for the next meeting or discussion.

Of course, not every situation can be foreseen and planned for. Each situation will vary. Many of these ideas can be applied in those unforeseeable circumstances, or altered to work in situations that are out of the ordinary.

CHAPTER EIGHT:
MEDIATION ADVOCACY & METHODS FOR EVALUATING CLAIMS FOR MEDIATION— BATNA, WATNA, AND ECONOMIC ANALYSIS

REPRESENTING CLIENTS IN MEDIATION

The degree to which attorneys prepare for mediation depends upon the nature of the case, at what stage the dispute is mediated, and how seriously counsel views the process. Some lawyers treat mediation as a nuisance foisted upon them by the courts. For them, it is merely another procedural stage in the action, and not an important one at that.[24] Others see mediation as a means of terminating the dispute on a positive basis for their client. These lawyers tend to prepare their clients and themselves as they would for trial. The latter put much more effort into their preparation and tend to get much better results. They understand that most civil claims are resolved without trial.

The amount of preparation varies with the type of presentation counsel and the client wish to make. The average presentation involves counsel delivering a prepared statement to the mediator in advance, followed by a substantial presentation during the first joint session. In these presentations, plaintiff's counsel generally makes a broader opening than the defense although the written presentations frequently are similar.

---

24. There are other reasons for lack of preparation. In some situations clients are unwilling to pay for the preparation time that counsel believes should be done. These are often defendant insurers in relatively small cases working on contingent fee arrangements. In cases where the mediation is voluntary or seen as the end game strategy, there are no proper excuses for lack of preparation.

Some plaintiffs, however, have prepared extensive opening presentations in an attempt to persuade the defense and the mediator. These include charts, slides, videotapes, objects, and even the introduction of experts. A few defense lawyers will use similar presentations to dampen the enthusiasm of the plaintiffs. Major presentations are not limited to business cases. More and more, we are seeing elaborate presentations in personal injury actions. We will discuss these types of presentations and how they affect the outcome below.

PREPARING THE CLIENT

Few clients are in the business of negotiating in the context of mediation; those who are do not need extensive preparation as to the process. These are claim representatives of insurance companies, third-party administrators, and self-insurers. Nevertheless, they need to be briefed on the individual case, the methods of the chosen mediator, and the approach counsel plans to take. Except for these professionals, clients need to be prepared for the process of mediation itself.

The client and counsel must decide how to approach the negotiation, what presentation to make, and who will make it. For instance, to what extent is the client going to participate in the opening remarks? Most mediators will encourage the client to speak. In personal injury actions, the impact of the injury on the client is an important issue. The defense will want to assess how the plaintiff will appear to a jury. The degree of persuasiveness of this sort of plaintiff will also affect the "reality testing" by the mediator. In a few personal injury cases, the actual defendant is brought to the negotiation. Usually, this results from his desire to apologize to the plaintiff and the family.[25] Sometimes, the

---

25. In a wrongful death case, defendant truck driver insisted upon appearing. This man, who looked like a football player, was in tears as he apologized, stating that his reaction to the event rendered him unable to drive any motor vehicle since the accident. This had the positive effect of taking at least some of the anger out of the negotiation and helped the parties in reaching a successful resolution.

defense produces the defendant just to have an impact on plaintiff's counsel. Like the plaintiff, the defendant's appearance also has the potential to significantly affect the jury.

In business and relational conflicts, the parties must be prepared to participate in the negotiation at every stage. This is more a matter of venting, clearing the air, and setting the stage for a successful negotiation than showing how the parties will impact the jury. Thus, counsel must spend time with the clients. A negotiation strategy must be created so that counsel and client are negotiating jointly with no surprises for either person.

For instance, in too many cases counsel will negotiate positionally, taking a tough stance. Later in the day, usually after much cajoling by the mediator, counsel must try to persuade her client to settle. Unless the client has been part of the strategy from the beginning, he may see his own lawyer as a turncoat. This will imperil what might have been an appropriate resolution.

The client must be prepared prior to the start of the negotiation. It is important that counsel not oversell the case. If the client's expectations are unrealistic, counsel should dampen them in advance. When the mediator later seems to be agreeing with counsel's evaluation of the case, the client is more likely to be satisfied with the proposed settlement.

PREPARATION BY COUNSEL

Counsel's degree of preparation depends upon the nature of the case and its status at the time of the negotiation. To the appropriate extent, counsel should have full knowledge of all important documents, all pre-mediation disclosures, medical reports, expenses, expert reports, and all evidence bearing on the outcome. All of this information must be digested and considered because it will affect the choices as to what to tell the mediator in the *mediation statement* which will be filed in advance of the negotiation. This preparation influences the decision as to what to disclose to the other side. Mediators tend to favor full disclosure in advance of the mediation. Some lawyers resist full disclosure because of their training and background in "hide the ball" litigation. A few believe that they have the smoking gun and will wish to keep it a secret. In my experience, the smoking gun almost never exists, and by the middle of the mediation the parties have made full disclosure.[26] It is a rare case that settles without full disclosure.

THE OPENING

This is counsel's opportunity to persuade the opposition and the mediator of the strength of her case and the client's willingness to enter into a serious negotiation to resolve the matter. Though these avenues seem to be contradictory, they must be traveled. The adverse party did not come to surrender.

The presentation, though strong on the facts and law favoring the party, should not be delivered in a needlessly offensive manner. The delivery should be earnest but restrained. It should be punctuated with words and phrases like, "We think we can prove this …" and "We understand that you disagree but …" or "We believe we have the law on this …"

Too often, counsel arrives with her "game face" on, coupled with a positional delivery which in substance and tone defeat the very aim of the negotiation. Usually, this is a tactic. Counsel seem surprised when the adversary replies in kind. If you prepare your client for a negotiation and not a street brawl, you need not worry about your client thinking you are too soft. More important, counsel needs to set a tone favoring a resolution, not impeding one.

When each side presents its best case but in the context of why a resolution is in the best interests of all, the right tone is created. The tone of negotiation is very important. If each side senses

---

26. Indeed, it has been my experience that lawyers, after spending enormous sums fighting disclosure during discovery, comply when the mediator asks them to disclose.

hope from the outset, it makes it easier for the mediator to do his job.

To prepare for the mediation, counsel must explore the types of presentations used at trial. We all know that persuasion in our society tends to be visual. Thus, visual aids that assist understanding are necessary to persuade. Today's lawyers are well versed in the use of computers. They use PowerPoint® presentations that interweave photographs, documents, and other materials.

Avoid the assumption that the other side knows the strong points of your case. Make the opposite assumption. Build a strong visual presentation. In our experience, a well-prepared opening will present some fact, issue, or approach that was not previously known by the adversary.

Also, avoid the assumption that you do not need to persuade the mediator. While the mediator may tell you not to bother, he is human. If he is persuaded, he will still remain neutral, but psychologically, the seeds of how you see the case being resolved will have been planted. Where you have hired the mediator to be an evaluative neutral, of course, you should try to persuade him.

EXHIBITS

The more your exhibits look like they were prepared for trial, the better. If you use charts to teach and persuade a jury, use the same format for the mediation. The exhibits should be large enough to be read with ease, and they should be factually accurate. Prepare to leave them with the other side during a caucus. You want to teach the other party the strength of your case.

More and more lawyers are using PowerPoint® presentations. They are not difficult to prepare. You can show slides on a screen that bring the case to life. You can mix pictures, charts, maps, and documents to have a seamless, powerful presentation.

If you fear a hole in your case will be uncovered, you must consider that in your preparation. Your opponent likely knows about the hole or will find it in the next round of discovery. Deal with it now as part of the negotiation.

In injury and death cases, video is a very persuasive tool. Do not shrink from preparing and showing the day-in-a-life video. Nor, if you are representing the defendant, should you shy away from videos that demonstrate that plaintiff's alleged injuries are less than claimed. Where you want to bring a subject to life, video and photographs are marvelous tools. Thus, to show a commercial process, location of an important place or fact, the terrain to be traversed, extent of damage to property, indeed any matter to be illustrated, use visual techniques.

A few lawyers have brought experts to the mediation. For instance, every lawyer thinks of herself as a physician—she can assess the injuries and the needed future treatment. This is absurd, of course, but attorneys keep believing it. In one case, plaintiff's lawyer brought two doctors with him. As part of the opening presentation, the doctors illustrated the injuries and the treatment. The defense was permitted to question and examine the experts privately in caucus. This tactic removed the non-medical speculation about the scope of the injury and its treatment, and led to a successful resolution of the claim.

Similarly, attorneys have brought experts in economics, patents, and a whole array of commercial subjects. If you bring an expert, she should be prepared to discuss the matter fully and even privately with your opponent.

If you approach the mediation as the occasion of resolution, just as you would the trial, your preparation and presentation will change radically as will your likelihood of success.

CAUCUS AND OTHER MEETINGS—WORKING WITH THE MEDIATOR

The standard mediation process pulls the parties apart after the joint session. Separated, the parties and their lawyers meet in a series of private meetings with the neutral who engages in shuttle diplomacy. Some lawyers see the neutral as a mail carrier, delivering demands and offers from one room to another. This is a mistake. You want the mediator to ask questions and make observations. Engage the mediator in a productive dialogue designed to test your case and your opponent's. This will advance the process toward resolution. If you make a mail carrier out of the neutral, you are taking on the entire burden for the success or failure of the negotiation. Put some of the burden on the neutral; that is why you hired him. Work with the mediator to create an approach to the talks. Suggest tactics to him and gauge his response.

A good mediator may want to meet privately with counsel, away from the client. This will give counsel an opportunity to discuss the case without having to look over her shoulder at the client. You should encourage meetings of this type, alone, and in tandem with your opponent. In an appropriate situation, the neutral may ask to meet with your client, outside of your presence. He will build to this point, not ask for it out of the blue. In capable hands, meetings of this kind can be very helpful. Indeed, in some cases the mediator will ask to meet with both or all clients without counsel. Where venting has already been achieved, and where a private meeting may break a deadlock, counsel should encourage it.

This runs counter to the lawyer's instinct to always be in control of the client. However, you will prepare your client not to surrender until you and he have discussed the matter after the private meeting. Client meetings are an excellent mediation tactic at the right time and in the right circumstances.

Another place to use the mediator is when the clients, and perhaps the lawyers, are close to an impasse. Ask the mediator for suggestions on how to restart the process. He may suggest a variety of strategies including setting a new range for the negotiation, hypothetical moves, and even a mediator-suggested resolution. Do not give up until all of these moves have been tried.

The mediator, with the patience of Solomon, must attempt to turn counsel toward reckoning the economic and human costs of a trial and appeal against a settlement. A BATNA analysis is one method. BATNA is the *best alternative to a negotiated agreement.* The mediator uses this litigation risk analysis in caucus when the parties are near an impasse. Although BATNA and WATNA (*worst alternative to a negotiated agreement*) analyses are frequently limited to the financial aspects of the negotiation (a matter we will illustrate below), it is important to recognize that parties often make decisions on other than strictly financial considerations. These intangibles are nearly impossible to quantify, but must be considered in any successful BATNA analysis.

For example, assume that a highly placed female executive is disappointed in the proposed pay increase that her company has offered for the next year. She believes that she is the victim of gender discrimination. She has entered into mediation with her employer in an effort to resolve the matter without resort to litigation. From the employer's perspective, the pay offer was low to reflect inadequate job performance. In assessing her BATNA, the aggrieved executive should consider her options. If she has a potential employer that is offering her satisfactory but not higher financial rewards and a more congenial workplace, her BATNA may be to leave her current employment and accept the other offer. People often prefer a more humane environment in the workplace to any other consideration, including cash.

The employer, on the other hand, may fear that the unhappy executive will resort to litigation. Even if counsel suggests that the putative plaintiff will not prevail, the company must consider the effects of the lawsuit in terms of bad publicity and low employee morale. Depending upon the circumstances, these considerations may weigh even more heavily than dollars. Thus, the BATNA may seem gloomy even if the likelihood of winning the lawsuit is better than 50/50. This party will want to stay at the negotiating table and negotiate an agreement.

As for our executive, if she has no happy job alternative in the offing, her BATNA may seem bleak, particularly if the economy is weak and/or her field of expertise is narrow. In this event, she will want to negotiate the best agreement that she can and remain at the job, at least for the time being.

Turning to a straight dollar analysis, assume that plaintiff in a simple injury case estimates that her verdict will be $15,000. She estimates the probability of that verdict at 80 percent, so her probable average verdict will be $12,000. Her litigation costs are about $2,000, lowering the amount now to $10,000. This must be further reduced by the cost of money. If the defense is now offering $7,500 in settlement, and if plaintiff rejects the settlement and does not collect anything until trial and a possible appeal, the plaintiff also loses use of the award money, a loss that could amount to $1,000. At this point, plaintiff's BATNA is about $9,000. If the cost of an appeal is added, plaintiff's BATNA drops into defendant's settlement range.

The defense analysis also starts with its view of a jury verdict. Say defendant believes that plaintiff will recover around $2,000. Its litigation costs will be $5,500. Its BATNA is $7,500. If the cost of an appeal is added, the BATNA rises to the $9,000 range. Although the figures used are artificial, the principle is apparent. The mediator may be able to show that the cost of going to verdict for defendant is greater than the settlement cost, and the recovery for plaintiff going to verdict is lower than what she would obtain in a settlement.

The obverse is called WATNA, the worst alternative to a negotiated agreement. The worst alternative is naturally a projected jury verdict in favor of the adversary. All the transaction costs, the opportunity costs, and human costs have to be added to the adverse result at trial. This is not a pleasant picture to paint.

CREATING A DECISION TREE[27]

Introduction

"What is this case worth?" This inquiry lies at the heart of virtually every settlement negotiation. The central goal of each party is to reach a result that makes the party better off than it would be if the parties kept on litigating. To bargain, we have to know the value of what we are bargaining over. When we know what a

---

27. ©1999 Daniel M. Klein. Dan Klein is a lawyer and professional mediator and arbitrator. Reprinted with permission from www.kleinmediation.com.

case is worth, we can negotiate with confidence. We can objectively weigh what the other side proposes and adopt positions that the other side is likely to take seriously.

It's often very hard to put a dollar value on a lawsuit, particularly an employment case. Unlike, say, automobiles, there are not so many essentially identical lawsuits that we can easily discern a "market price." The individual characteristics of employment cases tend to have, relatively speaking, great impact on their value. Change a few details in the fact record or substitute a new trial judge, and the value of the case can plummet or skyrocket. Lawsuits are full of uncertainty, and surprise twists abound. Often, we can't really predict with any accuracy how they will come out until they are over. Still, the process of valuing a lawsuit is so critical to settlement that we are always seeking ways to do so accurately.

One invaluable technique for determining the value of a case is the decision tree. A decision tree shows the various possible outcomes in a lawsuit and helps the parties evaluate the costs, risks and benefits of each outcome. In a typical lawsuit—where a plaintiff simply seeks to recover some amount of money from a defendant—a decision tree lists the most likely ways the case can come out and produces a weighted average of the results.

The discussion which follows shows how to build a decision tree to evaluate a sample case. When you've read through it, you will be able to use this technique to value your own cases. If you don't want to do the math yourself, however, there's a simple alternative. Click on "Create a Sample Decision Tree" at this web site, www.kleinmediation.com. You will find a program that does the work for you, by asking you a series of questions and then creating a decision tree using the information you provide.

Step 1: What are the possible outcomes?

The pages that follow illustrate the process of preparing a simple decision tree analysis in a typical employment discrimination case. The participants begin by sketching out, in broad form, the various "paths" that the case is likely to follow. Does the employer expect to file a summary judgment motion? If the case goes to trial, what is the range of probable verdicts the jury might return?

The decision tree described here would be prepared by the mediator and the employer in a "caucus" session. In our sample case, the defendant plans to file a summary judgment motion. If the motion is denied, the case will proceed to trial and the jury, if it finds for the plaintiff, will have a range of damages it could award. This example typifies a Title VII case, in which the plaintiff's back pay loss is relatively easy to calculate, but in which the jury might award compensatory and punitive damages, and will have great leeway in selecting the amount.

We begin to construct a decision tree by listing the possible outcomes that the case is most likely to reach. They become the branches on the decision tree. Our first illustration shows these possible outcomes. Each time there is more than one possible outcome, the tree branches out:

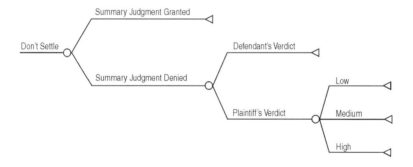

Step 2: What would be the cost of the possible outcomes?

Next, we estimate the cost to reach each outcome. Since our analysis in this example is from the employer's point of view, we include the employer's attorney's fees and expenses. For those outcomes in which the plaintiff wins, we add in the estimated amount of the jury verdict and the amount the court would probably award the plaintiff in attorney's fees.

In the second version of the decision tree, we have added the estimated cost of arriving at each possible outcome. We have made the following assumptions:

- If the employer were to win the case on summary judgment and successfully defend its victory on appeal, the cost to do so (in attorney's fees and expenses) would be $50,000.

- If the employer were to win the case at trial and successfully defend that victory on appeal, the cost to do so (again, in attorney's fees and expenses) would be $75,000.

- If the plaintiff survived the employer's summary judgment motion and won at trial, the jury would probably award the plaintiff back pay of $25,000. The jury might also award compensatory and punitive damages. We have condensed the total range of jury verdicts into three; that is, we have assumed the jury would reach one of only three possible verdicts. These are:

  - A modest ("low") award of back pay alone, or $25,000;

  - A more substantial ("medium") verdict that includes $75,000 in compensatory and punitive damages, for a total award of $100,000; and

  - A generous ("high") verdict that includes $275,000 in compensatory and punitive damages, for a total award of $300,000.

  - If the plaintiff prevailed at trial, the court would award the plaintiff $75,000 in attorney's fees and costs.

The following chart shows the amounts that we estimate the plaintiff would recover, in the event of a plaintiff's verdict:

Components of "Plaintiff's Recovery"

Type of Award	Back Pay	Compensatory & Punitive Damages	Plaintiff's Attorney's Fees & Costs	Total
Low	$25,000	$0	$75,000	$100,000
Medium	$25,000	$75,000	$75,000	$175,000
High	$25,000	$275,000	$75,000	$375,000

Once we add the employer's litigation expenses of $75,000 (the amount we estimated to take the case through trial and appeal), we see the total cost (to the employer) of the "low" plaintiff's verdict would be $175,000; the total cost of the "medium" plaintiff's verdict would be $250,000; and the total cost of the "high" plaintiff's verdict would be $450,000.

When we insert all of the outcome costs, our decision tree looks like this:

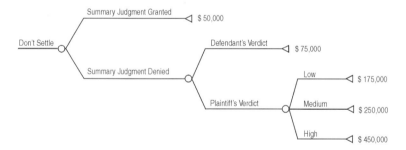

Step 3: What is the chance of each possible outcome?

Our next step is to estimate the chances of arriving at each possible outcome. The third decision tree shows the likelihood of each outcome as a percentage, and the percentages of all the possible outcomes at a given stage add up to 100. In our sample case, the employer has estimated it has a 75% chance of winning on summary judgment, but concedes that, if it loses the summary judgment motion, the plaintiff will have a 60% chance of winning before the jury. The employer has assigned probabilities of 40%, 50%, and 10% to the low, medium, and high verdict amounts.

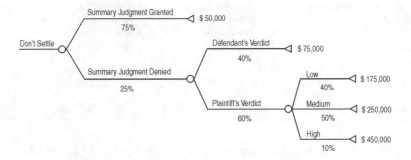

Step 4: "Rollback"

Having made all of these estimates, we then calculate the overall odds that each outcome would occur and multiply that percentage by the cost of the outcome. When we total up all the products, we get a "weighted" estimate of what the case will cost to litigate to conclusion. The following image shows these calculations, as performed by decision tree software. Like a spreadsheet, the software allows us to change any of the assumptions and see the modified result right away.

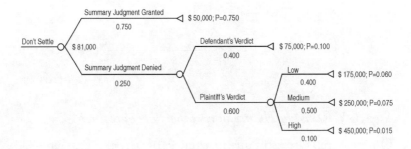

We can view the same set of calculations in a chart, or spreadsheet, such as this:

Outcome	Explorer's Litigation Expenses	Plaintiff's Recovery	Total Cost to Reach Outcome	Odds of Occurring	Expected Cost
Summary Judgment for Defendant	$50,000	$0	$50,000	0.750	$37,500
Verdict for Defendant	$75,000	$0	$75,000	0.100	$7,500
Low Verdict for Plaintiff	$75,000	$100,000	$175,000	0.060	$10,500
Medium Verdict for Plaintiff	$75,000	$175,000	$250,000	0.075	$18,750
High Verdict for Plaintiff	$75,000	$375,000	$450,000	0.015	$6,750
Weighted Cost					$81,000

Finally, Some Caveats

Decision tree analysis can be exceptionally valuable, but it has its limitations, too. The list of caveats about the usefulness of this analysis can go on and on. Here are a few:

- Decision tree analysis necessarily relies on very rough estimates about future events. The percentages and dollar figures can give a false impression of exactness.

- It doesn't necessarily take into account how wide or narrow the range of outcomes is, which can have an enormous effect on settlement decisions.

- It doesn't consider the parties' respective aversion to risk.

- As performed in these examples, it takes into account the employer's cost of litigation. The employer may ignore this cost, or claim to ignore it.

- Viewed from the plaintiff's perspective, the numbers will be lower since litigation costs won't be included.

A party may already have made up its mind about the value of the case before the analysis is run.

CHAPTER NINE:
MEDIATING SPECIAL TYPES OF CASES

PERSONAL INJURY CASES

The previous discussion about interest-based bargaining and joint problem solving applies in a wide variety of situations and cases. In many personal injury actions, however, it is difficult to break the old positional mold. Although the plaintiff is present with counsel, the defendant usually does not come to the mediation. Instead, only the defendant's attorney and the insurer's claims agent attend. The normal interplay between the parties is lost because only one of them is actually present; a joint problem-solving exercise is difficult if only one "side" is at the table. Also, there is no continuing relationship between the parties. The negotiators come together for this case only. Finally, the interests of the plaintiff diverge completely from that of the insurer. The former will indeed have a series of interests. The amount of the recovery determines how all his other interests will be met. The defendant's main interest is the cost of ending the action. This becomes the perfect backdrop for a positional bargaining negotiation and that is generally what occurs. This is true even late in the case when the parties are not withholding factual information.

In part, it is the nature of this particular beast. Both sets of lawyers are guessing what a jury is likely to do. The reasonable settlement value of the case is sometimes a question of "feel" and experience even if the economic facts are known. The transaction costs of continued trial preparation and the trial itself can be closely estimated by counsel. This data will have some effect on reaching an outcome if the parties' offers and demands come close to each other.

The mediator's efforts can be frustrated by the way the game is played. If counsel for plaintiff is familiar only with the positional approach, the mediator's efforts to have her focus on her client's real interests may be unrewarded. For instance, in these days of structured settlements, we know that where the plaintiff receives a large lump sum payment, about 70 percent of the recipients will be without funds in only two years after the settlement. That figure rises to 90 percent in five years.

One would expect that where the plaintiff is a young person or an individual unschooled in the ways of investment, his interests might lie in receiving a carefully structured settlement. Nevertheless, all too often counsel, for her own ego needs and bred by the positional game, will ignore the interests of her client and engage in the "dance" to "see the real number" before signing on. In part, this is driven by plaintiff's counsel's fee arrangement. The fee is often calculated using the defendant's total cost as the basis of the fee. The question so often heard is, "What will it cost the defendant?" not, "What will be the benefit to the plaintiff?"

For their part, defense counsel play the same game. Because no client is at the table, the claims representative, who plays this game several times a week, sees the negotiation in positional terms. From an interest point of view, she has no overstressed client for whom a trial would be a psychological disaster. She has no personal stake in the outcome. Thus, she is just another lawyer at the table. Only the plaintiff has a personal stake and a definable interest in human terms.

The claims agent has made an analysis of what the case is "worth" and an educated guess as to her company's exposure at a jury trial. Presumably she is aware of the actual dollar cost of the litigation to date, including counsel fees, expert fees, discovery, and the like. She must also calculate the cost of preparation for trial and the actual trial itself. This cost analysis is necessary to determine the actualization cost. For the insurance company representatives to engage in some sort of interest-based bargaining would require a general understanding of their employer's actual costs associated with an early settlement, a late settlement, and a full-blown trial in comparison to costs predicted for the case at hand. In other words, this case has to be put into the larger perspective of the company's results in settlements generally together with the analysis of the probable outcome of this case and the cost of that outcome.

The mediator can try to assist both parties in this negotiation. For instance, plaintiff's counsel will invariably "try" her case to the mediator from the opening statement onward. She will also be trying her case to the claims representative as well. If the claims representative is new to the case that may be a wise strategy because the opening statement will look and sound a bit like summation, complete with physical evidence and summaries of deposition testimony. Defense counsel's opening will also be an attempt to convince the mediator in the hope that he will convince the other party of the weakness of his case. In other words, instead of using the mediation to turn away from the problems of the litigation, counsel sees the mediation as nothing more than a part of the litigation. The result is that the bargainers are chiefly concerned with whether the other side has "moved enough" from their last position to be judged as negotiating in good faith. Most of the process is consumed with this idea.

For the mediator, the task is to make it clear that his role is not that of judge. To be sure, he will test the parties' statements and use their strengths and weaknesses to move them toward settlement options. But his role is to assist the parties in fashioning a settlement that is appropriate and acceptable to them, not to destroy his credibility by deciding who should prevail.

Time is a crucial element when getting to an accord. The mediator's best tactic is often to delay offers and demands. The plaintiff must spend time venting. Both parties must spend enough time in the negotiation effort to buy into the process. The passage of time has a psychological impact on the parties. The skilled mediator may be able to predict a narrow range for the outcome an hour or two into the process. Any suggestion of such an outcome at that early stage usually dooms the negotiation. At the four- or five-hour mark (or later) the parties frequently embrace the very outcome they had rejected earlier.

The range of outcomes depends on the parties, not the neutral. The outcome must be one that the parties can "live with." For the plaintiff, he must be able to handle closure emotionally as well as economically. For the defense, the outcome must make sense from the perspective of its business. The savvy neutral understands this and will not suggest an outcome that is outside the scope of last demands and offers. The mediator lets the parties create the boundaries through their bargaining. When they get stuck and cannot move any further, the mediator should suggest how the negotiating may be restarted. One option is to try to reset the range. That range should be within the parameters of the existing bargaining, but well beyond the place where the parties got stuck.

Thus, if the parties foundered with the plaintiff demanding $500,000 and the defense offering $100,000, it might be appropriate to reset the range at $250,000 and $350,000. This is a judgment call for the neutral. That is exactly what the parties pay the mediator to do—exercise good, informed judgment. If the restart is successful and the range severely narrowed, the case almost always will settle.

EMPLOYMENT MEDIATION

Mediating employment matters involving discrimination, harassment, retaliation, and the like require the neutral to use the most of his training to be empathetic and exercise good judgment at the same time.

These cases invariably involve an aggrieved employee or former employee. This individual may be the past president of the company, or more likely a person with a lesser job who feels that he has been treated shabbily by the employer. Feelings tend to run very deep in these cases. A woman who believes that she has been the victim of harassment; a man who believes that he was passed over because of his race; any person who believes that the company retaliated because of whistle-blowing, is a person who is angry and very emotionally involved. Frequently, these people are on a crusade to prove to their families, friends, and the public that they have been badly mistreated.

The company is seen as the enemy. Company officers are believed to be out to destroy the claimant. Often, the matter has engendered local or even national publicity. By the time the case gets to the table, the mediator is faced with a situation of all-out war.[28]

The mediator's neutrality will be sorely tested in these cases. The "victim" will believe to his core that evil things have been done to him. Nothing on earth is likely to persuade this individual that the facts are other than what he "knows." The plaintiff probably will have suffered some degree of public humiliation, and individuals within the company—the targets of some of these charges—also may have had their share of disgrace. It is a difficult, emotional situation for everyone.

The opportunity for venting is crucial in these cases. Some attorneys ask to skip the joint session, fearing that a face to face will be too difficult for their client. Yet it is that joint session which permits the individuals on both sides to express their strong feelings. Of course, the session must be carefully guided by the mediator so things do not get out of hand. Our experience is that if people are permitted to vent under controlled circumstances, they will hold enough back so as not to imperil the process. Their lawyers must prepare them in advance for this session so that they can take advantage of the opportunity. Lawyers are usually skillful at handling their clients in a manner that avoids a major blowup. By the time the joint session is over, the parties are aimed in the direction of getting to the business of finding ways to resolve the matter.

Most plaintiffs lose their enthusiasm for war. It is a very expensive undertaking, economically and emotionally. They cannot really get on with their lives until this matter is behind them. The skillful mediator knows this and will plan a private meeting with the "victim" late in the mediation. A similar conference will probably be necessary with the employer's representative who has been the focus of the charge. The plaintiff may be

---

28. Internal company mediation programs are designed to get the parties to the table before positions have solidified and negative publicity has occurred.

correct in his assessment of what occurred, but in the end, he must make a "business" decision as to what the resolution should be. It is the mediator's responsibility to make certain that all parties understand the financial and personal cost of continuing this sort of litigation.

In sexual harassment cases, the employee charged with the offensive conduct likely will be present. This creates another problem for the mediator. The company, if it believes the charge, may be ready to fire this person once the case is resolved. The person likely knows this, and he may be separately represented. It is probable in these circumstances that both the plaintiff and the company will want some cash contribution from this individual as part of the resolution. It is important that the mediator treat the charged employee as a separate party. This means the mediator should plan one or more separate caucuses with this individual. This person's interests are not the same as the corporation.

Apologies and good recommendations are also items for discussion in employment matters. Generally, the company will demand that the plaintiff leave his employment as part of the resolution. The plaintiff often will insist upon some form of apology and always asks that the company assist in his job hunt with a good recommendation. This should be centrally handled within the company. That is, someone should be assigned to receive all calls related to this employee. In that way, the recommendation given will be uniform.

These cases take great patience to mediate. The process may take many hours or several days. After all, we are asking a person who feels very much misused to resolve the case. On the other side, many employers feel that they are simply a target for an outrageous charge that lacks substance. Employers who feel this way may also be difficult to move to a resolution. The mediator must work patiently with their representatives to get to a business decision on the case. Remember, the charges in these cases may be against the corporation, but they involve the alleged actions of individuals. These people may be as angry as the "victim."

The mediator must maintain empathy for everyone in this fix. You can be empathetic for the plaintiff without agreeing that the charged conduct actually took place. Similarly, you can understand the position of the defendant without affirming the defense.

How do these cases settle? More than almost any other type of case, employment cases usually run out of gas.[29] The people come to some sort of compromise, perhaps to save their sanity, but definitely to get on with their lives.

---

29. This is not necessarily true of class action employment matters. Those cases are far less personal and do not yield to the emotional considerations involved in the individual case.

CHAPTER TEN:
DIVORCE MEDIATION

By Patricia A. Siuta[30]

INTRODUCTION

Mediation involving family disputes, particularly divorce, will generally involve highly emotional parties and issues. Next to the death of a loved one, divorce is one of life's most stressful events. It is not uncommon for one or both of the parties to cry or express anger during the mediation; occasionally, a party may even express thoughts of suicide.

People going through a divorce are usually not prepared for the difficult financial issues that they will have to face. Most find it difficult to make ends meet when there is one household to support. When two households must be established, it often results in the parties having a lower standard of living than they had prior to their separation and divorce. This can be particularly difficult to accept for the person who believes that he or she is the innocent victim, the one who is not seeking an end to the marriage.

For those who have children, the realization that they will be separated from their children for substantial periods of time can be devastating. During the mediation it is not unusual for parents to spend hours negotiating about who the children will be spending each holiday with, and who will be making decisions relating to the children's education, medical care, and religious upbringing.

A neutral mediating these types of conflict must be skilled in working with highly emotional parties, and must exhibit a great degree of patience. Divorce mediation frequently takes longer

---

30. Senior vice president, Resolution Resources Corporation. Ms. Siuta is an experienced mediator, arbitrator, and trainer.

than the mediation of other types of disputes, because of the emotions of the parties and the large number of issues that ordinarily must be resolved.

In addition to having training about the mediation process, mediators participating in divorce mediation should have knowledge of:

- Family law;
- The impact of family conflict on parents, children and other participants, including knowledge of child development, domestic abuse, and child abuse and neglect; and
- The impact of culture and diversity.[31]

COMMUNICATING WITH THE PARTIES PRIOR TO MEDIATION

A substantial number of mediations involving divorcing parties occur without the presence of attorneys. Some parties want to try to work out an agreement without attorneys to save money, while others do so because they are concerned that attorneys will make the process more adversarial. Even when the clients are represented by attorneys, it is not uncommon for attorneys to send their clients to mediation alone. In these circumstances the attorney will advise the client not to sign a mediation agreement until the attorney has had a chance to review it.

Parties who will be attending the mediation without attorneys should be advised that the mediator will not be providing any legal or financial advice and urged to obtain such advice prior to the mediation. Specific instructions, preferably in writing, should be provided to the parties regarding the information that should be brought to the mediation session. It is impossible to resolve issues regarding the disposition of assets and liabilities when the parties do not come to the mediation with information regarding these specific items. Many courts require the

31. American Bar Association, Model Standards of Practice for Family and Divorce Mediation, February 2001, Standard II, Commentary A.

preparation of a Financial Affidavit that lists each party's income, expenses, assets, and liabilities, as well as the expenses of the children. If the parties have prepared such a document, they should be advised to bring it to the mediation. If they have not, the mediator should ask the parties to compile this information prior to the mediation and bring it with them. Some mediators will send the parties a form prior to the mediation to facilitate the compilation of this information.

The mediator may also want to discuss who may be present during the mediation. Unfortunately, not everyone realizes that mediation is unlikely to be productive when a spouse brings his girlfriend or her boyfriend to the mediation, and expects this person to be present during the process.

SCREENING FOR DOMESTIC ABUSE

When the participants in mediation have a history of domestic abuse, the mediator must be aware of how this can affect the mediation process. Threats may even occur during the course of the mediation. For example, during a divorce mediation between unrepresented parties, a mediator observed that every time the wife spoke, the husband would open his sports coat, displaying a gun he had tucked into his waist band. This behavior was clearly designed to intimidate or threaten the wife. Faced with this behavior the mediator terminated the mediation, referred the wife to community services assisting abused women, urged the wife to obtain legal representation, and recommended that she pursue the matter in the courts, where a judge and jury would decide the issues.

Mediators handling divorce cases must be able to recognize family situations that involve domestic abuse so that they can take steps to protect the safety of the participants and themselves, and shape the mediation process.[32] Domestic abuse includes not only physical violence, but also severe emotional abuse encompassing issues of control and intimidation.

---

32. American Bar Association, Model Standards of Practice for Family and Divorce Mediation, February 2001, Standard X.

There is controversy within the mediation profession about whether it is appropriate to mediate divorce cases in which domestic abuse has occurred. Mediators have expressed concern about whether a person who has been the victim of such abuse can exercise self-determination. There is concern that in cases of domestic violence, the power imbalance may be so severe that meaningful negotiations cannot occur. Some believe that mediation is never appropriate when domestic abuse has occurred, while others believe that as long as the mediator has training in the area of domestic abuse, mediation should be available as an option. When the parties are represented by attorneys in the mediation, some of the concerns about the ability of a party to engage in a meaningful negotiation are alleviated.

Many divorce mediators employ a screening process designed to determine whether domestic abuse has occurred in the relationship. Screening may be done using a pre-mediation questionnaire or oral interview. If domestic abuse has occurred, these cases should only be mediated by those who have received specialized training.

If the mediator learns about abuse during the course of the mediation, he or she should be prepared to make referrals to appropriate community resources, if necessary.

TIMING OF THE MEDIATION

When mediation is scheduled while the parties are still residing together or shortly after their separation, the parties' emotions will often be more intense and volatile. The mediator may find that one party has not yet accepted the inevitability of the divorce. Although cases can be successfully mediated at this stage, it will be more difficult to assist the parties in reaching agreement, and the mediation process will generally take longer. If progress towards resolving all of the issues is not occurring, the mediator should consider suggesting to the parties that they try to reach agreement on preliminary issues, such as temporary child support and parenting schedules. The mediator may want to suggest that the parties reconvene in a month or two to consider the remaining issues, when emotions have subsided, and the parties have had time to adjust to the changes that have occurred in their relationship.

DEALING WITH EMOTIONS

The mediator should anticipate and prepare the parties for the expression of strong emotions during the course of the divorce mediation. The mediator can help manage these emotions and promote a meaningful dialogue by providing the parties with some communication guidelines when delivering his or her opening statement or monologue. An example follows:

> As you know, divorce is an extremely stressful event and most people going through a divorce experience a variety of emotions, including sadness, anger, and frustration. When people are filled with emotion, they often want to express how they feel. If you would like to express your feelings, you may do so during the mediation process. It can be difficult for the other person involved in the divorce to hear the expression of this emotion. I ask that each of you be patient and allow the other to talk about how he or she is feeling, if that is something the person wants to do. The expression of emotion, when done in a constructive manner, can often help the mediation process move forward. Frequently, people are unable to focus on the issues that need to be resolved, and engage in the problem solving process until they have a chance to express their feelings.

> I will give you an opportunity in a few moments to talk about the issues you would like to discuss today, and you may also express how you are feeling. Let me suggest that if you want to make progress in resolving the issues you came here to discuss, it is important that you be respectful of each other. Please use *I statements*, such as "I feel angry," rather than making statements that blame the other party. Each person will have the opportunity to speak without interruption, so that each will feel that he or she has had an opportunity to be heard, and so that I can understand what you have to say. It is also important to remember that our focus here will be to try

to reach an agreement regarding the issues that divide you. Therefore, after each of you has had a chance to speak, we will begin discussing the issues that have brought you here today.

After hearing from the parties, it can be helpful for the mediator to identify or reflect the emotions, so that the parties will feel heard and acknowledged. After the parties have had a chance to vent their emotions, the mediator should have an easier time moving them on to the problem-solving stage.

Other techniques that the mediator may want to use with very emotional parties include:

- Separating the parties by meeting privately in caucus;

- Taking frequent breaks;

- Scheduling multiple shorter sessions, instead of working on all issues at one session, to give the parties a chance to work through the issues and their emotions at a slower pace;

- Referring the parties to a therapist or counselor so that they will have help in working through their emotions;

- Recommending that a party obtain legal counsel, if a party is not represented; and

- Suspending the mediation until a later date.

CONFIDENTIALITY

A family mediator has the same obligations regarding maintaining the confidentiality of the mediation process as any other mediator. Although a mediator is required to maintain confidentiality, "[a]s permitted by law, the mediator shall disclose a participant's threat of suicide or violence against any person to the threatened person and the appropriate authorities if the mediator believes such threat is likely to be acted upon."[33]

---

33. American Bar Association , Model Standards of Practice for Family and Divorce Mediation, February 2001, Standard VII, Commentary C.

Information that a child is being abused is generally considered an exception to the mediator's responsibility to keep information learned during the mediation confidential. Mediators should check the laws in the state in which they practice to learn about their reporting requirements. The mediator may be required to report this information to child protection services.

ISSUES INVOLVING CHILDREN

The most difficult issue for parents to resolve is usually the issue of child custody and the time the children will spend with each parent. When discussing these issues, the mediator's choice of words can aggravate or ameliorate the parties' emotions. For example, the mediator should avoid using the word "visitation," whenever possible, using terms such as "parenting schedule," or "time the children spend with each parent."

The mediator has the responsibility to promote the consideration of the interests of children affected by the agreement.[34] He or she may have to raise issues regarding the needs of the children when the parties are not addressing those needs. The mediator must be aware of the impact of a child's age on the feasibility of particular parenting arrangements or schedules. For example, if the parents are considering a parenting schedule that would require a young child to alternate nightly between each parent's home, the mediator should engage the parties in reality testing, because such an arrangement is not considered appropriate by child development specialists, and is unlikely to be approved by the court. The mediator may suggest to the parties that they consult with a child development specialist if they have questions regarding age appropriate custodial arrangements. Parents should also be reminded that child support, custody, and parenting arrangements need to be approved by the court.

Most states have child support laws or guidelines with which mediators will need to be familiar. It is also helpful to have

---

34. Academy of Family Mediators, Standards of Practice for Family and Divorce Mediation, Standard VI. B.

knowledge of how often and under what circumstances child support can be modified after a divorce decree is granted.

CHECKLIST OF ISSUES

There are so many issues that require resolution in the typical divorce mediation that many mediators use a checklist to ensure that all necessary issues have been considered. In the joint session the mediator should ask the parties or their representatives to identify the issues they would like to resolve during the mediation. After those issues have been addressed, it is a good idea for the mediator to review other areas that typically require resolution to ensure that all issues have been identified and resolved. A divorce mediator's checklist should include the following:

Assets:

- Marital residence;
- Other real estate;
- Retirement accounts;
- Bank accounts, money market funds, and certificates of deposit;
- Securities such as stocks, stock options, and bonds;
- Trusts;
- Life insurance;
- Business ownership and assets;
- Personal property;
- Intellectual property; and
- Vehicles.

Liabilities:

- Credit card accounts;
- Debts;
- Mortgages; and
- Alimony.

Child Issues:

- Parenting arrangement;
  - Legal custody;
  - Physical custody; and
  - Parenting schedule: weekdays, weekends, holidays, and vacations;
- Child support;
- Health insurance;
- Education arrangements and costs; and
- Children's investments and accounts.

Tax Consequences

DRAFTING THE MEDIATION AGREEMENT

A divorce mediation agreement is generally longer and more detailed than other two-party mediation agreements. It can be helpful to develop and use a form to help expedite the drafting of the agreement. For example, many mediators prepare a list of all the holidays to review with the parties when discussing and drafting the parenting schedule.

Unlike many other types of disputes that are mediated, the parties in a divorce mediation will often have a continuing relationship, because of parenting and financial support responsibilities. This continuing involvement often leads to future conflicts. A common way of addressing this is for the parties to insert into the agreement a provision that they will return to mediation prior to going to court if there is conflict in the future.

The mediator should carefully contemplate how future conflict relating to a person's failure to perform some agreed upon task might be avoided or minimized, and have parties consider procedures for dealing with such nonperformance. For example, if a participant in the mediation is to remove all personal property from the marital home by a certain date, the issue of what the other participant may do with the property if it is not removed should be discussed and set forth in the agreement.

Changes in the parties' circumstances, such as a parent moving out of state, can also lead to future conflict. When drafting the mediation agreement, the mediator should anticipate potential changes in the parties' circumstances and determine whether the parties wish to address them in their agreement.

Finally, if the parties' attorneys do not attend the mediation session, consider including a provision providing for review of the mediation agreement by the attorneys prior to the agreement being finalized.

STANDARDS OF PRACTICE

The Model Standards of Conduct for Mediators are contained in appendix C. In addition to these standards, the American Bar Association adopted Model Standards of Practice for Family and Divorce Mediation (hereinafter "Model Standards") with which mediators practicing in the area of divorce should be familiar. Although they are aspirational only, they describe good practices. The majority of the Model Standards restate practices that are common to all mediations. Those that are specific to the area of family and divorce mediation have been noted therein.

In addition to the ABA, the Academy of Family Mediators has established similar Standards of Practice for Family and Divorce Mediation.

CONCLUSION

Mediating divorce cases provides many challenges for the mediator. With attention to the issues described above, however, the mediator can successfully assist the parties in reaching resolution. Divorce mediators often experience great satisfaction in assisting parties in resolving issues that intimately affect every aspect of their lives. For a family involved in conflict, mediation offers the best prospect of resolving their dispute in a quick, confidential, and inexpensive manner, thereby helping to conserve the parties' assets and income. It often has the added benefit of helping to "repair" the parties' relationship, at least insofar as reopening or facilitating respectful communications between the parties.

CHAPTER ELEVEN:
ETHICAL CONSIDERATIONS

Some states have implemented specific guidelines for the ethical conduct of mediations. All mediators must read and follow these guidelines; however, they should do so in light of other guidelines that they as a professional are required to follow. For example, attorneys are bound by the code of professional conduct adopted in the state in which they practice. There is an ongoing debate as to whether lawyers who act as mediators are also acting in their capacity as lawyer, and are therefore bound by rules pertaining to the practice of law. Until that issue is clearly decided, it is best to assume that all standards that normally apply in one's professional capacity also apply while mediating. Appendix C is a code of professional conduct for mediators suggested by the American Bar Association with help from the Society of Professionals in Dispute Resolution (SPIDR—now merged into a group called the Association for Conflict Resolution), and the American Arbitration Association (AAA).

There are numerous ethical issues that mediators face in different circumstances. By following basic standards, however, most situations can be handled with a minimum of worry. There are several basic rules mediators should follow in order to avoid ethical dilemmas. The mediator should:

- Remain impartial and avoid conflicts of interest;
- Encourage self-determination and voluntary actions;
- Maintain confidentiality; and
- Ensure the fairness of the process.

These four basic obligations help the mediation process run smoothly and avoid unnecessary complications. It is hard enough to help others resolve problems; keeping ethical standards high is essential to maintaining trust in, and respect for, the process.

IMPARTIALITY/CONFLICTS OF INTEREST

This obligation means impartiality in both word and deed. Like a judge or an arbitrator, a mediator must avoid even the appearance of impropriety. For this reason, a complete conflict check should be done before a mediator is agreed upon. Have there been any past relationships between the proposed mediator and either party, its representatives, parent companies, or affiliates? If so, how close are the ties? Is the history something the parties are comfortable waiving? Does the mediator's employer or law firm have any relationship? This issue has become quite significant as law firms set up mediation groups within the firm. The American Bar Association (ABA) has proposed a new rule (Rule 1.12) that allows firms to provide a "screening wall" for the mediating attorney in any potential conflict-of-interest representation the firm undertakes. The idea is to screen mediating (or arbitrating) attorneys from receiving any potentially biasing information from the firm. Several courts have upheld the screening wall as long as it is shown to be effective.[35] In addition, it makes sense to get a clear waiver of any potential conflict in the Agreement to Mediate.

Of course, it is inappropriate for a mediator to take on any dispute after the mediation where the mediator would represent one party against the other party from the mediation, even if the issues appear to be unrelated. It is possible that some of the information gained in the mediation could become useful to the attorney in this subsequent case. This problem would be obvious where the parties mediate a dispute over the merger of two companies and then years later one party wants the mediator to represent it when the parties decide to dissolve the company. It would make sense to hire the attorney/mediator who was most closely involved in merging the companies, but the information that the attorney gained in the mediation would provide an unfair advantage later.

---

35. *Chapman v. Chrysler Corp.*, 54 F. Supp. 2d 864, 866 (S.D. Ind. 1999); *Poly Software Int'l, Inc. v. Su*, 880 F. Supp. 1487, 1494 (D. Utah 1995).

In addition, there may be problems where mediators refer cases to lawyers. Such referrals happen often when parties attend a divorce mediation unrepresented and then need an attorney to draw up the final divorce agreement. Mediators, especially those who are lawyers, should be careful not to refer cases only to one lawyer or law firm. Again, the appearance of impropriety is the issue. Many states and model rules specifically address this issue and prohibit exclusive referrals.

During the process, maintaining impartiality is also essential. Sometimes it is quite difficult not to agree with one party (the wife who is being left or the employee who clearly got passed over for a well-deserved promotion), but allowing those feelings to interfere with neutrality while running the process is deadly. The parties see it and lose trust in the mediator's ability to let them make their own decisions. New mediators are always certain that they know the "right" answer after opening statements or after the first caucus or joint session. Pushing the parties toward a settlement is just as much a showing of partiality—it is still taking sides; it just happens to be your side instead of one of the parties'.

Another issue that affects neutrality is when one party's representative is ineffective. Is it okay to help the representative present her evidence and arguments? Is it okay to be persuasive in a caucus with the other party on issues that you know the representative would not be persuasive about? It is the mediator's duty to help the parties figure out how best to negotiate. But finding that fine line between helping to negotiate and making the deal for the parties is difficult.

In order to maintain neutrality, the mediator must keep in mind that it is the parties' problem, not the mediator's, and that this process most likely is the fairest method for these parties to resolve their dispute. The mediator should work hard to ensure that power plays are minimized or eliminated, reality test the unreasonable party, and empower the weaker party to talk and make requests. He must also help the parties find objective standards on which to base their decision or case law that shows the likely outcome at trial. Of course, there is a definite line not to cross—practicing law or providing professional advice. But it is appropriate to make suggestions for how the parties can resolve differences of opinion or find a basis for a settlement offer. For example, in the employment case, it is appropriate to ask the parties what the standard is for determining discrimination in the state or jurisdiction, and send them to attorneys to do that research and provide definite advice. It is not appropriate to go research the standard and case law for them.[36]

SELF-DETERMINATION AND VOLUNTARINESS

The point of mediation is to help the parties find their own best solution to their problems. For this reason, there has been much emphasis placed on the need to allow the parties to decide the outcome for themselves. Whether they settle anything, everything, or nothing must be left to them. This issue has become problematic as courts have started mandating that cases be sent to mediation. One of the first questions asked by the parties is how this process can be voluntary when the courts have required them to be there and to participate in good faith. Voluntariness does not go to attendance. Instead, it goes to resolution. What resolution, if any, is up to the clients. The mediator must make it clear that he will not tell the parties what to do in the mediation process and that the parties are free to leave at any time. They do not waive or impair their right to go to trial and have their case decided by a jury because they went to mediation first. Of course, if an agreement is reached in mediation, the parties are bound by it just as they are by any contract, and the mediator must make sure that the parties understand when the process goes from nonbinding to binding.

---

36. There are many attorney-mediators who do this research on their own for background before the mediation or who know the answers as a matter of expertise. There is great controversy over whether providing these answers constitutes practicing law by the mediator. In the author's opinion, it is best to stick to mediating and let the lawyers practice law. In a case where legal standards, jury verdicts, and sticky legal matters are being contested, the parties should be encouraged to have lawyers with them at the mediation.

As long as the parties go through the process in good faith, the courts have accomplished their goal. Even cases that do not settle at the mediation session have a good chance of settling before trial. Statistics are not clear enough to quote as to whether settlement is reached because of things said and done in mediation or merely because most cases settle before trial. The general consensus seems to be that mediation helps speed the case toward settlement, if for no reason other than that it forces the parties to talk about settlement, usually earlier than they might have otherwise.

Self-determination goes more toward who makes the resolution decision. In order to ensure self-determination, it is the mediator's obligation to make sure the parties understand the process and are both willing and able to participate in it. This obligation makes an effective *mediator's monologue* essential. Mediators must make sure the parties understand that the mediator is there to act as a neutral third party, not a decision-maker; that the mediator will not give legal or financial advice; that the process is to be kept confidential (and the exceptions to confidentiality); that the process can be terminated at any time by the mediator or any party; that the parties are free to seek legal counsel or professional advice at any time; and the impact of reaching an agreement at mediation.

Self-determination becomes an issue in several contexts. First, where there is a clear power imbalance, mediation may not be the best resource. For example, in a case of domestic violence, the victim spouse could agree to almost anything in the hope of appeasing the abuser. In court, however, the abuser can be kept away from the victim and the victim can be awarded things he or she would never ask for in a negotiation out of fear. There are many initiatives and training courses that help mediators learn to balance power, even in extreme cases. Those specially trained mediators may be asked to mediate disputes where there are great power differences or issues of possible threats. But where a mediator feels that a party cannot reach a fair decision, or can be better protected by the court system, the mediator should stop the process. And when a mediator feels less than adequate to handle the problems before him, he should either refer the parties to a mediator with special skills or refer them back to the court for protection.

Next, where there is an issue of capacity to negotiate or to reach agreement, self-determination is an issue. There are questions of temporary incapacity (*e.g.*, a party who shows up drunk) and of permanent incapacity. Where capacity is only a temporary problem, a mediation may be postponed. Of course, the issue of fairness to the other party in rescheduling can be a problem, but rescheduling at least once happens all the time. In cases where permanent capacity is at issue, the mediator has a tougher decision. Can the case be mediated at all? Should a guardian be appointed? Who should take on that task? Will the court provide better protection? Because the mediator is in charge of the process, it is incumbent on the mediator to make sure the process is fair, regardless of whether agreement is reached.

As discussed in the section on impartiality, mediators are faced with a tough decision when one party's representative is less skilled or knowledgeable than the other. Self-determination is another reason mediators must stop short of helping parties win their cases—every party has the right to choose their representative. Just as in court, bad representation makes for bad outcomes. Mediators must allow the parties to decide for themselves how much to allow their attorneys to affect the outcome of the case. Because mediation is a client-driven process, it has a better chance than the court does to even out the playing field—intelligent clients may make up for less-than-stellar attorneys.

An issue that the mediator might face is whether to be a party to an agreement that seems unfair. Mediators have an obligation to make sure that the agreements reached are not illegal or impossible to execute. For example, a mediator who happens to be a tax attorney will know that a divorce agreement which specifies tax consequences prohibited by the tax code cannot be upheld by the court. Through reality testing and sending the parties off to examine the tax consequences, or to seek expert help, the mediator can help the parties modify their agreement so it is valid.

But where the parties agree to terms that the mediator feels are patently unfair, the mediator's role is far from easy. Parties can agree to anything they wish as long as it is not illegal or otherwise harmful (criminal activity, child abuse, etc). They can agree to things that courts could or would never order. The mediator's job is to make sure the parties understand what they are agreeing to, the consequences of their actions, and the impact on others from the agreement. After the mediator is confident the parties understand the consequences and are competent to reach an agreement, then it becomes the mediator's choice whether to sign the agreement. The mediator cannot prohibit the parties from entering an agreement that he feels is unfair; he can only make his objections known and refuse to sign it. Of course, the mediator is faced with how to make objections known without voicing an opinion that hinders the parties' right to self-determination.

CONFIDENTIALITY

In most mediation agreements, there are provisions stating that the parties agree to keep everything said during the mediation confidential. There are further provisions stating that the mediator will keep everything confidential and that the parties will not subpoena the mediator to testify to anything that happened or that was said during the mediation.[37] There are usually stated exceptions to this confidentiality requirement, which are discussed in more detail below. During the process, mediators maintain confidentiality in several ways. The first way for mediators to protect the parties' interests in confidentiality is to make sure they do not reveal information gained in caucus to the party not present during the caucus. In addition, mediators have a strong requirement that information gained in the mediation will not be revealed to any person not present during the

---

37. A sample mediation agreement is attached as appendix A: Resolution Resources Corporation Agreement to Mediate, (*see* ¶¶ 3–5). In addition, appendix D contains a discussion of ethics from the Georgia Office of Dispute Resolution.

mediation without permission from the parties or an order from the court.

The mediator has an obligation to each party and to the integrity of the process. As discussed earlier, the purpose of caucus is to talk about things that could or should not be discussed jointly. This discussion includes reality testing, discussion of real interests and needs, and evaluation of offers and counteroffers. If the mediator were to reveal these points to the other party without permission, pretty soon no one would trust the mediator with confidential information. On the other hand, where one party reveals something in caucus that is essential to the other party's ability to make an informed decision, but refuses to allow the information to be conveyed to the other party, the mediator has a dilemma. Should the mediator tell them anyway? No. That clearly violates confidentiality. Should the mediation be terminated? Maybe. But that does not ensure that the other party ever finds out the information. And what do you tell the parties when you terminate?

When does the information reach the point where the mediator has an obligation to reveal it? Unfortunately, there are no clear guidelines. Obviously, if someone is in danger, the appropriate persons (authorities, intended victims) should be told. If someone is contemplating committing fraud, the obligation is much less clear. Of course, no one wants to be a party to fraud, but what do you do? The answers are not readily apparent; we must consider each issue and think through what our actions should and will be. There are statutes that guide mediators in making the decision on whether to reveal confidential information. Also, the Uniform Mediation Act sets out specific instances under which confidentiality is not protected:

- An agreement reached during mediation that is evidenced by a record signed by all the parties;
- Information available to the public under open records laws or made during a mediation that is open to the public;
- A threat to inflict bodily injury;

- When mediation is intentionally used to plan or commit a crime or conceal ongoing criminal activity (What does this mean for the obligation to reveal completed crimes?);

- Situations of child abuse; and

- Claims of professional misconduct or malpractice by a party or representative (*i.e.*, mediators may reveal confidential information to protect themselves against claims of malpractice).

While the act waives the mediation privilege in the above circumstances, it goes on to state that a mediator may only disclose whether a mediation occurred, who attended, whether settlement was reached and communications evidencing abuse, neglect, abandonment, or exploitation of individuals. It appears, then, that one must look to one's conscience and other professional obligations to determine whether there are other instances in which information should be revealed.

Most professionals have an obligation under their own standards or applicable case law to reveal threats of bodily injury, and many would argue that planned crimes must be reported. Finding that happy medium between maintaining confidentiality and the integrity of the process versus doing your civic duty is a tough call. The general rule is that you have to follow your instincts. If they tell you to run, run. If they tell you to call the authorities, call.

After completion of the mediation, different issues arise. Third parties are not bound by the confidentiality agreement, and in fact are often quite interested in learning what went on in a mediation and, especially, in the outcome. Co-defendants often want to know what their settling co-defendant paid for purposes of divvying up verdicts. Plaintiffs in similar circumstances want to know what their employer paid a settling employee in similar circumstances. Generally, courts uphold the confidentiality of the process and do not require parties to reveal what went on in a mediation.[38]

In addition, confidentiality issues arise when parties try to bring in evidence of what happened during a mediation at a court hearing. Mediation is clearly considered a settlement negotiation, and therefore prohibited from being discussed in court. Generally, courts are quick to prohibit the introduction of such information. Problems have been raised, however, where courts have a requirement that parties negotiate in good faith. Some courts have forms for the mediator to fill out stating whether the parties did, in fact, negotiate in good faith. Where the mediator reports that one party did not, the courts are in a dilemma: how to find out what went on in order to decide on appropriate sanctions without requiring anyone to breach their obligation of confidentiality. There does not seem to be any satisfactory solution at this time.

More problems arise when parties arrive at an agreement in mediation and then disagree on the details when their lawyers later try to write up the final papers. When one party files a motion to enforce the agreement (usually in the form of a Memorandum of Understanding created during the mediation), the other party subpoenas the mediator to testify that there was no agreement or that the terms are different. Usually, the courts have upheld the phrase in the mediation agreement that states that a mediator will not be asked to testify in any subsequent court hearings.[39] Recently, however, a magistrate judge, who also happens to be a well-respected mediator, issued a thorough opinion holding exactly the opposite.[40] In *Olam v. Congress Mortgage*, Judge Wayne Brazil held that, where both parties

---

38. *Folb v. Motion Picture Industry Pension & Health Plans,* 16 F. Supp. 2d 1164, 1176 (C.D. Cal. 1998).

39. *See* cases cited and discussed in "Keeping the 'R' in ADR: How Olam Treats Confidentiality," *Alternatives,* December 1999 (CPR Institute For Dispute Resolution, New York, NY), Dec. 1999, at p. 187.

40. *Olam v. Congress Mortgage,* 68 F. Supp. 2d 1110 (N.D. Cal 1999).

wanted the mediator to testify, and where the value of the mediator's testimony would outweigh the harm to the values that underlie the mediator's confidentiality privilege (first revealed *in camera* and then, if valuable, in open court), the mediator could be compelled to testify. The judge made it clear that state law rules of evidence applied because state law controlled the substantive issues.

It appears that states that adopt the Uniform Mediation Act would come to a conclusion similar to the court in *Olam*. The act creates strong protections for confidentiality and specifies that each person must waive the privilege of confidentiality as to his own communications except in very unique circumstances. Those circumstances include trying to avoid or reform a contract arising out of mediation, and showing involvement in a felony, child abuse, or professional malpractice. As in *Olam*, the court will first conduct an *in camera* (private) hearing to determine whether the information can be obtained elsewhere or is essential to the decision before the court.

LIABILITY OF THE NEUTRAL

There have been occasions when parties have sued mediators or arbitrators on the grounds that they committed malpractice in conducting the ADR process. In almost every instance, the courts have dismissed the lawsuits. In arbitration, the courts hold that arbitrators perform a quasi-judicial function and therefore should have immunity as judges do when trying cases.[41] The exception to this immunity is where it can be shown that the arbitrator is involved in fraud, coercion, or corruption,

---

41. *Buyer's First Realty, Inc. v. Cleveland Area Board of Realtors*, 745 N.E. 2d 1069 (Ohio App. 8th Dist. Cuyahoga 2000); *Olson v. National Association of Securities Dealers*, 85 F. 3d 831 (C.A. 8 Iowa 1996).

not just when there was "serious error" in the arbitrator's decision, forcing the court to overturn the decision.[42]

Mediators likewise are rarely held liable, but not necessarily for the same reasons. In mediation, of course, the mediator is not deciding anything for the parties or binding them to anything. Therefore, there is little to hold him liable for. Generally the mediator will not be liable unless he acted in bad faith, with malicious purpose, or in willful and wanton disregard of human rights, safety, or property.[43] There have been a few instances, however, where the courts found that the mediators were acting as attorneys, giving legal advice, and therefore should be held to the same standards as attorneys or should be held liable for the unauthorized practice of law if they are not attorneys.[44]

---

42. *Cohen Highley Vogel Dawson v. Bon Appetit Restaurant*, 44 O.R. 3d 73 (1999), as discussed in David I. Bristow, Q.C. and Jesmond Parke, *The Gathering Storm of Mediator & Arbitrator Liability*, 55-OCT Disp. Resol. J. 14, 16 (2000).

43. *Postma v. First Federal Savings & Loan of Sioux City*, 74 F.3d 160 (C.A. 8 Iowa 1996). *See also Wagshal v. Foster*, 28 F.3d 1249 (C.A. D.C. 1994), extending quasi-judicial immunity to a court appointed mediator. The court in *White v. Horton*, 1 Mass. L. Rptr. 213, 1993 WL 818800, *5 (Mass. Super. Ct. 1993) found no such immunity for noncourt ordered mediations.

44. *See* Russell Engler, *And Justice for All—Including the Unrepresented Poor: Revisiting the Roles of the Judges, Mediators, and Clerks*, 67 Fordham L. Rev. 1987, fn. 95 (1999) (listing several states' rules and treatment regarding mediation legal boundaries). But see John W. Cooley, *Shifting Paradigms: The Unauthorized Practice of Law or the Authorized Practice of ADR*, 55-OCT Disp. Resol. J. 72 (2000) (making the argument that ADR and mediators' roles are misperceived and rules should be expanded to allow for more latitude in this area).

CHAPTER TWELVE:
CO-MEDIATION AND OTHER TYPES OF MEDIATION

There are times when the task of mediating a case would be better performed by more than one mediator. Most often co-mediators are called for in cases of unusual complexity, in cases where a specific expertise would be helpful in resolving the dispute, and in cases involving a multiplicity of parties. Complex cases and complex party situations tax the time and resources of a single mediator. Understanding the issues and working with the parties may require more than one neutral. This is particularly the situation in cases that involve tangled factual issues with heavy resort to documents.

Multiparty cases call for the help of an experienced co-mediator because of the need for caucuses with each party or interest group, the "shuttle diplomacy" required, and the difficulty of formulating and keeping the parties to an agenda. Other instances in which co-mediation is popular occur when the issues of the case involve the need for expertise. For instance, in construction, medical malpractice, intellectual property, and other similar situations, it will be useful for one of the neutrals to have sufficient understanding of the area so that the statements, positions, and interests of the parties will be well understood. Often the expert is not an experienced mediator, so a co-mediator with great mediation experience, but perhaps with little or no subject -matter experience, is brought in. Moreover, there is frequently a need in a caucus to throw some cold water on a party position that will not withstand analysis. This "reality testing" is always part of the mediator's job. It cannot be done effectively if the neutral lacks a fundamental understanding of the matter under discussion.

There are a few other occasions in which co-mediation is widely used. It is difficult for mediators to get adequate feedback on their work skills. That settlements are being achieved is not a measure, in itself, of the ability of the neutral. Often, mediators working for the same company or organization will co-mediate to further the learning in their craft. In addition, new mediators can advance their training by co-mediating with experienced ones.

Co-mediation does not mean, however, that one mediator dominates the proceeding while the other sits in a corner and observes. An actual sharing of the workload is most desirable. The co-mediators should divide the proceeding in a convenient manner and each act as a neutral with the moral authority that a mediator may have. In this connection it is important that each mediator speak early in the session. To accomplish this, the co-mediators must learn to work together and not at cross-purposes. They must meet and discuss how they will handle the case, agree on a proposed agenda and strategy, and decide how the workload will be divided. They must be courteous and not step all over each other at the sessions. This will require a degree of restraint from both persons.

During the mediation session, the co-mediators should state in the opening statement that they may caucus with each other if developments warrant such action. It may be necessary to do this to set the actual agenda they will advance to the parties, after having heard the opening statements delivered by the parties. It may also be necessary to meet to talk about strategies and changes in strategies necessitated by surprising developments at the session.

MULTIPARTY MEDIATION

Multiparty mediation includes a wide variety of situations. It can simply be a case involving more than two parties or it can be the most complex type of "meeting," involving hosts of warring interest groups ready to do public battle.

In the former situation, the cases with a number of parties, the techniques of mediation previously discussed apply. It likely will be necessary for the mediator or co-mediators to have more frequent caucuses with individual parties in order to keep the sessions on track. Indeed, some mediators have only one general session before doing all the remaining work in private caucuses.

This has the benefit of keeping the emotional level low, but it does not effectively engage the parties in joint problem solving. The total caucus approach, as it were, is one where the mediator carries the maximum burden for fashioning the settlement options and then "selling" them to the parties. If the objective is to have the parties engage in a joint effort, general sessions are required.

In the "meeting" situation, the mediator(s) is taxed heavily. This is a conference more than a mediation in the traditional sense. Thus, hosts of issues have to be dealt with before the session is convened. The convening party must be interviewed with care to determine the purpose of the conference if chaos is to be avoided. Each participant should also be interviewed in advance in an attempt to create a common agenda. Even though the parties are likely at war, arriving with a common agenda and a common set of objectives for the conference may spell the difference between success and failure. Issues such as those listed below need to be resolved:

- Location of the conference;

- Shape of the table;

- Where each party sits in relation to the others;

- The order in which topics will be discussed;

- The order in which each party speaks; and

- The availability of documentary material.

The mediators must ascertain what their role truly is. They may be hosts whose job is to give some sort of public airing to a thorny political issue. In the alternative, they may be involved in a substantive process, the purpose of which is to gain agreement among the parties on some or all of the issues.

Each of the parties or their representatives must be consulted to ascertain their hopes and fears relating to the issues under discussion and the conference itself. The mediator(s) should work in advance to remove surprise. Each party should be made to feel that the mediator(s) is truly neutral and cares about the interests of each of the parties. If the trust of the parties can be gained in advance, the public meeting may be a successful, if limited, means of achieving objectives. Without proper preparation, public conferences among widely divided parties soon degenerate into little more than proclamations of the positions of the parties.

FACT-BASED MEDIATION

Fact-based mediation is based on the premise that disputes arise due to a lack of knowledge of the facts or misperception of the facts. Frequently, this type of mediation is used in construction disputes. The mediator gathers all possible facts about the case. He then writes a report on the facts as he sees them. The report sets out the deficiencies of and problems with each party's case. Each party gets a different report, setting out his own deficiencies but not those of the other party. In the report the mediator projects a possible jury or arbitrator's award based on his independent analysis of those facts.

The mediator estimates the costs of arbitrating and/or litigating. He then recommends a settlement that takes all factors into account.

- All information is confidential.
- The mediator will not testify in any further proceedings.

CHAPTER THIRTEEN:
ARBITRATION

Arbitration is the form of alternative dispute resolution most widely used in industry. Many contracts contain arbitration clauses stipulating that the parties must resort to arbitration rather than litigation to resolve disputes arising under the contract. Such clauses are found in collective bargaining agreements, particularly those involving public workers. They are also found in most construction contracts. The securities industry mandates the use of arbitration in disputes between the broker and the customer or employer. Professional sports organizations also widely require arbitration to decide salary disagreements between players and club owners.

Arbitration may be court annexed or private, binding or non-nonbinding, and be governed by rules created by the parties themselves or by rules prescribed by the administering private organization. For the most part, we will be discussing private, binding arbitration. The parties enter this process either through a contract reached before any dispute has arisen or by a contract negotiated in order to resolve a particular case.

Few people have any real understanding of what arbitration is, how it works, and how it is different from other forms of dispute resolution. At its simplest, arbitration is a means of resolving disputes where parties choose a neutral, often expert, decision-maker or panel of decision-makers, and agree to be bound by that person or panel's decision. The process of arbitration varies from simple to complex, depending upon the parties' actions and the agreement they enter into regarding arbitration.

In his article, "Arbitration vs. Mediation—Explaining the Differences," John W. Cooley sets out the history of arbitration and explains how it differs from mediation:

> An amazing number of lawyers and business professionals are unaware of the differences between arbitration and mediation. Their confusion is excusable.

In the early development of the English language, the two words were used interchangeably. The *Oxford English Dictionary* provides as one historical definition of arbitration: "to act as formal arbitrator or umpire, to mediate (in a dispute between contending parties)." The States of Edward III (1606) referring to what today obviously would be called a commercial *arbitration* panel provided: "And two Englishmen, two of Lombardie and two of Almaigne shall (be) chosen to be mediators of questions between sellers and buyers."

Modern labor relations statutes tend to perpetuate this confusion. As one commentator has observed, some statutes, referring to a process as "mediation" describe formal hearings, with witnesses testifying under oath and transcripts made, require reports and recommendations for settlement to be made by the neutral within fixed periods, and either state or imply the finality of the "mediator's recommendations." In one statute the neutral third parties are called, interchangeably, mediators, arbitrators and impasse panels.

The Federal Mediation and Conciliation Service (note the absence of "arbitration" in its title) performs a basic arbitration function by maintaining a roster from which the Service can nominate arbitrators to the parties and suggest "certain procedures and guides that (the Service believes) will enhance the acceptability of arbitration."

The National *Mediation* Board (emphasis added) performs important functions in the promotion of arbitration and the selection of arbitrators for the railroad and airline industries.

Libraries also assist in perpetuating the arbitration/mediation definitional charade. Search under "mediation" and you will invariably be referred to "arbitration." In the midst of this confusion—even among congressional draftsmen—it is time to explain the differences between the processes.

The most basic difference between the two is that arbitration involves a *decision* by an intervening third party or "neutral"; mediation does not.

[Also], the two processes are generally employed to resolve two different types of disputes. Mediation is used where there is a reasonable likelihood that the parties will be able to reach an agreement with the assistance of a neutral. Usually, mediation is used when parties will have an ongoing relationship after resolution of the conflict. Arbitration, on the other hand, is generally appropriate for use when two conditions exist: there is no reasonable likelihood of a negotiated settlement; and there will not be a continuing relationship after resolution.

If the two processes are to be used in sequence, mediation occurs first, and if unsuccessful, resort is made to arbitration. Viewed in terms of the judicial process, arbitration is comparable to a trial, and mediation is akin to a judicial settlement conference. They are as different as night and day.[45]

In the United States, arbitration historically was not well regarded by the courts. They felt that arbitration was a form of judicial ouster. In addition, it allows forum shopping through a choice of decision-maker, and it allows circumvention of the protections provided by the courts. The courts were concerned that the parties would lose the protections designed into the Constitution by choosing arbitration.

---

45. John W. Cooley, "Arbitration vs. Mediation—Explaining the Differences."

In 1925, however, the Federal Arbitration Act was enacted.[46] This statute provides that parties may agree to be bound by arbitration decisions and that the courts will not review or change the decisions except in the most limited circumstances. While the FAA does not confer federal jurisdiction, it does preempt state laws that restrict arbitration in cases involving interstate commerce.[47] Except for contracts of employment for workers engaged in foreign or interstate commerce, the FAA applies to all arbitration agreements with two limitations: the transaction or contract must involve interstate commerce or a maritime agreement;[48] and to the extent that law and equity provide grounds to revoke any contract, the same grounds apply to an arbitration agreement in a contract.[49]

Today, after many years of following the FAA and state statutes governing arbitration, the courts mostly have deferred to arbitration decisions. Because there has been a strong movement by

---

46. 9 U.S.C. §§ 1 et. seq.

47. *Southland Corp. v. Keating*, 465 US 1, 104 S.Ct. 852, 79 L.Ed.2d 1 (1984). *But also see Volt Information Sciences, Inc. v. Board of Trustees of the Leland Stanford University*, 489 US 468, 109 S.Ct. 1248, 103 L.Ed. 2d 488 (1989), in which the Supreme Court held that the FAA does not preempt state law or agreed-upon rules about how the arbitration should be conducted. (The parties agreed to apply California law to deciding the dispute; California law allowed the court to stay the arbitration pending related litigation involving the parties and others not involved in the litigation where "there is a possibility of conflicting rulings on a common issue of law or fact.")

48. In *Allied v. Bruce Terminix Cos. v. Dobson*, 513 U.S. 265, 277 (1995), the Supreme Court interpreted § 2's "involving commerce" phrase as implementing Congress's intent "to exercise [its] commerce power to the full." In *Circuit City Stores, Inc. v. Adams*, 121 S.Ct. 1399 (2001), (U.S.), the Supreme Court interpreted not § 2, but § 1, which exempts "contracts of employment of seamen, railroad employees, or any other class of workers engaged in foreign or interstate commerce." In that case, the Court found that Congress did *not* intend to exempt all employment contracts from coverage under the FAA; it merely intended to extend the exemption to transportation workers.

49. 9 U.S.C. § 2.

industry to require that arbitration be agreed upon before any dispute has arisen (for example in consumer contracts or employment agreements), the courts have taken it upon themselves to ensure that basic protections are offered to those who agree to arbitrate disputes that arise in the future. For example, when employers require employees to arbitrate employment disputes, controversy arises over who should pay for the arbitration, how to select the panel of arbitrators, how much discovery should be allowed or required, and what remedies the arbitrator may award.

ADVANTAGES

There are numerous reasons to choose arbitration over litigation, mediation, or any other form of dispute resolution. And, just as with every form of ADR, there are many disputes for which arbitration is not the best choice.

Confidentiality

Arbitration is private. Unless the parties choose to file court papers or to leave an arbitrator's decision unsealed when it is filed with the court for enforcement purposes, everything done in arbitration can be kept confidential. The hearings may be closed to any outsiders. The parties may agree to keep the decision confidential. Documents used in the arbitration may also be kept from outsiders. For many companies, this feature is an attractive way to ensure that others are not encouraged to file similar claims or lawsuits.

Speed and Cost

Arbitration can be as simple or as complex as the parties make it. It can take place within days of an incident or years, depending on the parties' actions. If discovery is minimal and the witnesses are available, arbitration can be inexpensive and quickly concluded.

Finality

Many people believe that the greatest advantage of arbitration is its finality. The grounds for judicial review are so limited that most arbitration decisions are not appealed. In most cases, once an arbitration hearing is complete, the arbitrators have thirty days to make a decision; the judgment, if any, is paid and the dispute is over. This reason is why so many personal injury disputes are arbitrated. The facts are often straightforward or not in dispute, and the injured party needs the funds immediately rather than after years of trial and appeals. For the insurance company, cases are cleared from their files much more quickly than cases that are tried to a jury and then appealed.

Control

When we take cases to court, there are rules and procedures to follow. The judge and jury have their own way of doing things. In arbitration, the parties may choose to follow pre-written rules and procedures, such as those provided by Resolution Resources Corporation or the American Arbitration Association, but they are not required to do so. They can redesign the process as they deem appropriate for each dispute, choose rules that the arbitrators are required by contract to follow, and even stipulate as to the form of the arbitrator's decision. They can require that the arbitrator follow a particular state's laws, or not be bound by the law. The parties can agree on a time and place for the hearings. They can voluntarily limit discovery and hearing time. They can make the process as formal or informal as they wish.

Choice of Decision-Maker

One of the reasons courts historically disliked arbitration is precisely the reason so many parties choose it. In court, each case is assigned randomly to a judge. It may be heard by a judge who has no experience at all in hearing or trying cases dealing with the complex subject matter of the particular dispute. Certainly a jury would not be expected to understand the nuances of complex litigation. But in arbitration, the parties can choose arbitrators who are experts in the field in which the dispute arises. Historically, construction disputes have been arbitrated for precisely this reason. Parties do not want to waste hours trying to explain the complex construction process and its attendant relationship issues to a jury when they can hire arbitrators with years of construction practice who immediately understand the issues. Also, the expert decision-maker's experience will help them fashion a remedy that makes sense in the particular context.

Informality/Lower Stress

While most lawyers are comfortable in a courtroom, few clients are. Arbitration is much less formal—no one has to rise to question witnesses or make arguments; arguments about how a witness is being questioned or whether evidence is admissible are discouraged. By design, the process should be less adversarial. As much as possible is agreed upon in advance. This "friendlier" approach reduces tensions and allows everyone to concentrate on the dispute and its resolution.

DISADVANTAGES

Lack of Sympathy

Arbitrators, as experts in the field, are rarely as sympathetic as juries. Like judges, they have vast experience and will not be swayed by emotional testimony, legal maneuvers, or attempts to recover overinflated awards. Arbitrators do not often award punitive damages.

No Precedential Value

As a private, out-of-court resolution, the arbitrator's decision cannot be used as precedent. In the labor field, arbitrators publish decisions and arguments are made based upon them, but the decisions themselves have no power to bind a court or future arbitrator. Thus, when presented with a case where there is a contract provision to interpret, and its interpretation will affect hundreds of other contracts not presently involved in the dispute, arbitration probably is not the best option.

Cost

While arbitration cost is minimal in most cases, it still is an issue. Litigation requires only filing fees, expenses, and attorneys fees. The decision-maker's salary and administrative fees are paid from our taxes, not by individual litigants. Attorneys fees and other costs associated with prolonged litigation historically made arbitration a more economical alternative. Recent trends toward requiring full discovery, allowing arbitrators to hear motions, and to hold extensive and complex hearings before three-judge panels, however, have increased the costs of arbitration dramatically. In some instances, arbitration can become more expensive than litigation. In those cases, parties have to decide whether the advantages of arbitration outweigh the extra cost.

Limited Remedies, Protections, and Rights

Issues still remain as to whether arbitrators may award attorneys fees, punitive damages, or other remedies. The FAA does not specify the scope of awards, but allows an award that could not be granted by a court (§ 12(a)(5)). The parties may agree, then, that the arbitrator can award punitive damages, even if state statutory or case precedent do not allow them in similar cases.[50] Generally, the parties should set out in the arbitration agreement what types of damages the arbitrators can and cannot award.

Also, whereas court rules and statutes specify rights to discovery in litigation, generally no such protections are built into arbitration agreements. Discovery is conducted as the parties agree or the arbitrators order. Some people feel that this lack of right to discovery jeopardizes the rights of the parties to have a fair hearing, especially the plaintiff, who has no access to the defendant's records. Also, since the parties cannot go before a jury or appeal to a court, some feel that arbitration unfairly deprives them of their constitutional rights. Of course, many of these concerns are alleviated where the parties agree voluntarily to arbitrate a

---

50. *Mastrobuono v. Shearson Lehman Hutton, Inc.*, 514 U.S. 52 (1995); *Davis v. Prudential Securities, Inc.*, 59 F.3d 1186 (11th Cir. 1995) (also holding that attorneys fees are awardable only if provided for in the arbitration agreement).

dispute after it arises and negotiate from roughly equal footing on how the process will be conducted.

THE PROCESS

Arbitration follows a specific process. While arbitration may vary in formality and is widely adaptable, the basic elements are identifiable and predictable.

The Demand or Submission

Arbitration is initiated by a *demand* if there is a pre-dispute arbitration clause. It is initiated by a *submission* if the parties agree to arbitration after the dispute arises. Some arbitration providers require a formal filing and provide specific forms for filing. Others provide only a simple Agreement to Arbitrate form[51] and allow parties to file more formal complaints specifying the issues only if necessary. The parties to an arbitration are referred to as *claimant* and *respondent.*

The Answer

Some providers allow parties to answer the complaints set forth in the demand or submission within a specified time (usually ten days). Unlike court rules, failure to answer is not construed as an admission. Instead, if the party does not answer, all claims are treated as denied. The *answer* should also set forth any counter-claims the respondent might have.

Pre-Panel Issues

Issues such as whether the claims are arbitrable should be addressed next. The court addresses these issues unless the agreement leaves that decision to the arbitrators. Whether parties should be joined or claims consolidated should also be considered. There is no right to joinder or consolidation in arbitration,

---

51. *See* appendix F, Resolution Resources Corporation Contract for Arbitration and CPR's Model Agreement for Parties and Arbitrator.

but courts may order it in their discretion. Where the arbitration should take place may also be an issue. Finally, if an injunction needs to be issued by a court to preserve the status quo pending the outcome of the arbitration, it is generally sought at this stage.

Selecting the Arbitrator or Panel of Arbitrators

Choosing the best arbitrators is a daunting task. Unlike most other processes, this choice will affect the entire outcome of the case. This individual or group will control scheduling issues, procedures at the hearing, and the outcome of the case, with limited right to appeal. They are instructed to reach a "fair and equitable" decision, not limited by precedent.

The first issue to resolve is choosing the number of arbitrators. Usually the choice is one or three arbitrators. Originally, most arbitrations under AAA rules and other commercial processes used three arbitrators. One method is for each party to choose one arbitrator and then have "their" arbitrators chose the third. This way, each party will have one unrelated party who will see the dispute from his perspective (a general contractor usually will choose an arbitrator with general contracting experience) who could take his expertise and perspective back to the decision room and convince the "neutral" arbitrator to see things his way. This process works well in cases where there are complex issues and where information presented could easily be misunderstood without some expertise. The parties should agree when using this method that all the arbitrators will be designated as neutrals and that there will be no ex parte communication with any of the arbitrators.

There has been a move toward choosing just one arbitrator in many cases, especially the simpler ones involving less money. If the parties can agree upon this choice, they will save time and money. Generally, AAA suggests one arbitrator if the amount in controversy is under $1 million and three arbitrators if the amount is over $1 million. If the parties cannot agree on the arbitrator(s), many arbitration codes allow the courts to make that decision. Arbitration providers also have provisions for choosing arbitrators for indecisive parties without resort to the courts.

Often the suggestions for choices of arbitrators come from the arbitration provider. The provider will be careful to conduct a conflict check to make sure the arbitrators have no affiliation with or interest in any of the parties which might bias their decision. One of the few grounds for overturning arbitration decisions is that the arbitrator was biased.[52] The standard for determining partiality is

- The extent and character of the personal interest;
- The directness of the relationship;
- The connection of that relationship to the arbitration; and
- The proximity in time between the relationship and the arbitration proceeding.[53]

Clearly, given this standard, the appearance of partiality is important—if it could look bad, arbitrators must get a waiver from the parties or step down. Hopefully, any potential conflicts will be revealed before the process begins. A proposed Code of Ethics for Arbitrators in Commercial Disputes, drafted by the American Bar Association with the help of representatives from AAA and SPIDR, provides guidance on conflicts of interest and other ethical responsibilities of arbitrators. It is attached as appendix E.

---

52. *See, e.g., Arista Marketing Associates, Inc. v. Peer Group, Inc.*, 720 A.2d 659 (N.J. Super A.D. 1998), where the third arbitrator was held to be biased because he was an attorney who had met with one of the parties and prepared documents pursuing dissolution of the party's corporation as an option to the outcome of the arbitration or settlement agreement. *But see Team Scandia, Inc. v. Greco*, 6 F. Supp. 2d 795 (S.D. Ind. 1998), holding that an arbitrator was not biased where he had represented a manufacturer who was a third party to the dispute, the relationship had been disclosed prior to proceeding, the representation had been three years prior, and the arbitrator's decision did not reflect favorably upon the manufacturer.

53. 9 U.S.C. § 10 (a) (2). *See ANR Coal Co., Inc. v. Cogentrix of North Carolina, Inc.*, 173 F.3d 493 (C.A.4 N.C. 1999).

Pre-Hearing Conference

Especially in complex cases, it is common for the arbitrator (or chief of the panel) to hold a conference, either in person or by telephone with the parties to discuss important issues. Some of those issues include:

- Definition of issues—specifically what the arbitrator will be deciding, so there is no question that the decision is the one the parties seek;
- Timing—how long it will take to prepare; how much hearing time will be necessary;
- Discovery—what can be agreed to; how much is necessary;
- Stipulations—evidence, witnesses, authentication of documents;
- Motions—some arbitrators, especially in complex cases, hear motions similar to those that would be made in court; and
- Prehearing briefs—are they necessary? When should they be filed? Will the parties be allowed to respond?

More often, the arbitrators hold a final prehearing conference after discovery is complete and just before the hearing is to take place. The purpose of this conference is to narrow issues, stipulate to certain facts, and take care of any issues that arise. This conference is very much like the pretrial conference held by many judges.

Preparing for the Hearing

All attempts are made to streamline preparation. In complex cases, the parties prepare a list of probable witnesses and documents to be produced, with a synopsis of the subject of their testimony. Depositions are taken as agreed to in the prehearing conference. Witnesses are prepared. Hearing notebooks are created. These notebooks include all the documents that may be introduced, in numerical order, usually with a table of contents. Each party is presented with a notebook, as is each arbitrator.

Hopefully, this preparation will make the hearing go as smoothly and quickly as possible.

The Hearing

The FAA requires that parties in an arbitration have an opportunity to be heard, to present material evidence, and to cross-examine witnesses. These basic rights are designed to ensure the parties due process. In affording these rights, however, the arbitrators are given broad discretion. Formal rules of evidence do not apply unless the parties specifically agree to use them. Generally, the only objections made in an arbitration are that evidence is not material to the dispute or relevant to the issue. These relatively vague terms encourage the admission of all evidence, including hearsay, with the admonition by the arbitrator that she will "take it for what it's worth." Courts have upheld this broad discretion as necessary to "rid the proceeding of formalities and expedite it in line with the very aims of the arbitral process."[54]

The hearing is conducted in much the same manner as the trial would be, but dispensing with unnecessary formalities. Some examples of differences between jury trials and arbitrations include:

- In arbitration, witnesses may be questioned while the attorney is seated rather than standing.

- Documents in arbitration are considered "self-authenticating," which means that if, for example, a document dated June 10 purports to set out the agreement of the parties, no witness is required to testify as to what it is and when it was written unless there is an objection to its authenticity.

---

54. *Reed & Martin, Inc. v. Westinghouse Electric Corp.*, 439 F.2d 1268 (2d Cir. 1971).

- Affidavits or depositions may be introduced instead of witnesses, as long as there was an opportunity for all parties to question the absent witness in person.

- Charts, graphs, and other summaries of voluminous data are encouraged. While the supporting data can be made available to the other parties and the arbitrators if necessary, any attempts to condense material and reduce hearing time are encouraged.

- It is common for the arbitrators to ask questions of the witnesses. The purpose is to clarify information or to have the witnesses address a conflict in testimony. Arbitrators generally refrain from taking over the examination.

- The arbitrators will not hesitate to let the parties know that they have heard enough from one witness or on a particular topic, and ask that the parties move on or avoid repetition.

Opening statements are made, witnesses are questioned and cross-examined (both by the parties and often by the arbitrators), evidence is presented, and closing statements are made. Sometimes post-hearing briefs are ordered to clarify issues or summarize extensive hearing material.

Experts are allowed and encouraged in arbitration. However, their testimony may be handled quite differently than it would be at trial. First, the arbitrators rarely need the background that would be provided at trial, so the testimony is often much shorter and more technical. Next, the arbitrators are free to ask questions, and usually do. Finally, it is not at all unusual for both parties' experts to testify at the same time or at least to be allowed to listen to each other's testimony, and respond to each other directly rather than separately through lawyers' examinations like they would at trial.

Post-Hearing

At the conclusion of the hearing, the arbitrator or chief arbitrator will ask if everything has been presented. If so, the hearing will be concluded and the arbitrator(s) will begin considering her decision. If the parties wish to submit briefs, a witness remains to be heard, or a document needs to be presented at the request of the arbitrator(s), a time will be set for that information to be received. After all information is received, the hearing is closed. Like a bench trial, an arbitration decision is not rendered immediately. By contract, the arbitrator(s) generally has thirty days to render her decision.

The Award

The arbitrator's award will be in writing, setting forth whatever specifics the arbitrator deems necessary to conclude the case. It may include simply a statement that Party A owes Party B $X. Or it may be more detailed, including when, where, and how payment should be made, and whether interest is due. Unlike a judge's detailed findings after a bench trial, the arbitrator's award often contains no reasoning. Arbitrators take this approach to minimize costs—spending time on reasoning out the award seems to be a waste of time and the parties' money. A benefit to this approach is that it renders the decision virtually unappealable. A court cannot second-guess an arbitrator if the reasoning is not present.[55] In the highly specialized field of labor law, however, awards are reasoned and published. And because parties usually want to know how the arbitrators reached their decision, many arbitration rules and providers are moving toward requiring arbitrators to provide a reasoned decision, however brief.[56]

---

55. In *Greene v. Hundley*, 266 Ga. 592, 596, 468 S.E.2 350, 354 (1996), the Georgia Supreme Court overturned a Court of Appeals decision vacating an arbitrator's award because it contained no findings of fact. The court held that "A reviewing court is prohibited from weighing the evidence submitted before the arbitrator, regardless of whether the court believes there to be sufficient evidence, or even any evidence, to support the award." *See also Valentine Sugars, Inc. v. Donau Corp.*, 981 F.2d 210 (C.A. 5 La. 1993).

56. Center for Public Resources Rules for Non-Administered Arbitration, Rule 14.2, RRC Rules for Arbitration, 13.2.

An arbitrator is free to craft any remedy she deems just and equitable. This standard is quite different from the decisions made by courts. Arbitrators have much more flexibility in making awards; the fact that a court could not have awarded the relief granted by an arbitrator is not grounds for refusal to enforce an award.[57] Arbitrators are encouraged to follow the law, but their decision will not be overturned unless they exhibit a "manifest disregard" for the law.[58] In other words, making a decision that follows the "spirit" of the parties' agreement rather than the letter of the law is perfectly acceptable.[59]

What kinds of awards arbitrators are allowed to make is unsettled. Usually it is best if the parties agree in advance to remedies they would like the arbitrator to consider. Generally, courts have held as follows:

- Monetary relief and specific performance are allowed.

- Punitive damages may be allowed under the FAA and many state laws, but it is better to specify in the

---

57. O.C.G.A. 9-9-13; UAA § 12(a)(5).

58. *Montes v. Shearson Lehman Bros., Inc.*, 128 F.3d 1456 (11ᵗʰ Cir. 1997), vacating an award but stressing that "manifest disregard of the law" does not mean vacating awards when arbitrators misinterpret or incorrectly apply the law; it only applies when arbitrators are conscious of the law and deliberately choose to ignore it. (While arbitrators are free to apply the "essence of the agreement," rather than strict legal principles, this standard makes it difficult for reviewing courts to decide whether arbitrators are applying contract law or "the essence.")

59. 9 U.S.C. § 10. *See Atlanta Gas Light Co. v. Trinity Christian Methodist Episcopal Church*, 231 Ga. App. 617, 500 S.E. 2d 374 (1998); *In re Cragwood Managers, L.L.C (Reliance Insurance Co.)* 132 F. Supp.2d 285 (S.D.N.Y. 2001) "If a barely colorable justification for an arbitration award exists, the award should be confirmed."

arbitration agreement to avoid the issue of what is allowed under the arbitration rules and statutory law.[60]

- Costs and expenses are awardable unless the agreement provides otherwise.

- Attorneys fees are awardable only if the agreement so provides.

- Prejudgment interest is awardable if the agreement so provides.

- Post-judgment interest is awardable from the date of entry of the award.

An arbitration award may then be taken to court to confirm the award or to vacate it. If confirmed, the award becomes enforceable as would a court judgment. Usually confirmation is unnecessary because parties pay the award and conclude the dispute.

---

60. In *Mastrobuono v. Shearson Lehman Hutton*, 514 U.S. 52 (1995), the Supreme Court overturned a decision upholding the application of New York law preventing an arbitrator from awarding punitive damages where the arbitration agreement allowed the award. Had the parties agreed to preclude punitive damages, the Court also would have upheld that agreement. *See also Mitsubishi Motors Corp. v. Soler Chrysler-Plymouth, Inc.*, 473 U.S. 614, 105 S.Ct. 3346 (1985). There does seem to be disagreement about whether arbitrators can award punitive damages unless the agreement specifically allows for the award. *See Ryan v. Kontrick*, 304 Ill. App. 3d 852 (1999) (Parties' contract specified use of Illinois law but failed to specify punitive damages award in agreement; therefore, arbitrator could not award punitive damages); *but see Faiyaz v. Dicus* 245 Ga. App. 55 (2000) (Arbitrator did not exceed his authority in awarding punitive damages based on his finding of fraud and intentional breach where arbitration agreement did not specify the allowable award but included choice of Georgia law); *Complete Interiors, Inc. v. Behan*, 558 So.2d 48 (Fla. App. 5 Dist. 1990) (Arbitrator exceeded powers by awarding punitive damages and attorneys fees under Florida law absent contractual or legislative authority).

Vacating Awards

State statutes and the FAA specifically set forth limited grounds for vacating awards. The grounds set out in § 10 of the FAA include:

- Where the award was procured by corruption, fraud, or undue means;

- Where there was evident partiality or corruption in the arbitrators, or either of them;

- Where the arbitrators were guilty of misconduct in refusing to postpone the hearing upon sufficient cause shown, or in refusing to hear evidence pertinent and material to the controversy, or of any other misbehavior by which the rights of any party have been prejudiced; and

- Where the arbitrators exceeded their powers, or so imperfectly executed them that a mutual, final, and definite award upon the subject matter submitted was not made.[61]

Where an award is vacated, and the time within the agreement required to make the award has not expired, the court may in its discretion direct a rehearing by the arbitrators.

Section 11 of the FAA allows an award to be modified or corrected where there was an evident miscalculation or material mistake in a description of a person, thing, or property referred to in the award (if the arbitrator clearly added two numbers incorrectly or cited the wrong address for the house to be sold); where the arbitrators decided a matter not submitted to them; or where the decision is imperfect in form, not affecting the merits. Courts interpret these circumstances extremely narrowly, almost always refusing to review any arbitration decision unless it clearly requires modification.

---

61. 9 U.S.C. § 10 (a).

Modification is rare, and vacation by a court is even rarer. The issue of whether to vacate becomes compelling, however, when courts are asked to enforce decisions that are contrary to public policy, especially in the labor field. Generally, the Supreme Court has limited public policy review to situations where "the contract as interpreted would violate 'some explicit public policy' that is 'well defined and dominant, and is to be ascertained by reference to the law and legal precedents and not from general considerations of supposed public interest.'"[62] How this ruling is applied by the various circuit and state courts in specific cases, especially nonlabor cases, varies from court to court.

VARIATIONS ON A THEME

Like all alternative dispute resolution processes, arbitration can be modified in a myriad of ways to meet the needs of the parties. Below are just a few of the possibilities:

Court-Ordered or Nonbinding Arbitration

Nonbinding arbitration seems to be a misnomer, because the basic premise of arbitration is to agree to let someone else decide the dispute and abide by that decision. The problem with courts ordering parties to arbitration, however, is that a court cannot require them to waive their right to trial before a judge or a jury. So, in the hopes that a reasoned, speedy opinion will help the parties resolve their differences, many courts have set up a mandatory arbitration program where the parties are not bound by the decision of the panel. Although run much like an abbreviated arbitration (usually just an hour or so), these arbitrations are much closer in substance to *neutral evaluation*, discussed in chapter 5.

---

62. *United Paperworkers International Union, AFL-CIO v. Misco, Inc.* 484 U.S. 29, 108 S.Ct. 364, 98 L.Ed. 2d 286 (1987)(holding that the public policy against drug use and operating dangerous machinery was not clearly defined enough for the court of appeals to overturn an arbitrator's decision reinstating plaintiff when he was discovered in the back seat of his automobile with a marijuana cigarette in the front ashtray).

High/Low Arbitration

This type of arbitration is just your typical arbitration so far as the arbitrators know. The parties, however, have made an agreement that creates parameters for the award. The parties might agree, for example, that the most the defendants will pay is $100,000, and that the least they will pay is $10,000. In this example, if the arbitrators find for the defendants and award nothing, the plaintiff at least receives $10,000. If the arbitrators go to the other extreme and award $300,000, then the defendant is protected from such a high verdict. The arbitrators are not told of this agreement, since it could influence their decision.

Med/Arb

Med/Arb is a process where parties attempt to resolve their dispute through mediation, but agree in advance that if they cannot, the mediator will switch hats and make a final, binding decision. How the process works depends on the parties. In some cases, the mediator/arbitrator decides at the close of the mediation session. In others, formal testimony or presentation of evidence and arguments are made after mediation fails. The advantages are that the parties know the problem will be resolved quickly and completely, and that the mediator has an extra "carrot" to help the parties reach resolution because they know they will relinquish control if they do not. The disadvantages are that people are usually reluctant to share damaging or personal information when they know the neutral may consider it in making the final decision.

Med/then Arb

This process is designed to eliminate the potential problem of the mediator changing hats and having information an arbitrator might or should not have. In Med/then Arb, one person mediates and, if the matter is not resolved, a different person arbitrates. To save time and money, the arbitrator might sit in and hear opening statements, but she will not hear any further discussions. The same advantages apply—the case will be decided one way or another very quickly. The disadvantage is paying two different neutrals.

Arb/Med

Arb/Med sounds like it could not possibly work, but it alleviates many of the problems associated with other processes. First the case is arbitrated. The arbitrator (usually just one) makes a decision and puts it aside. Then either the arbitrator or a different person mediates the dispute. The parties are motivated to settle because they know a decision is waiting if they do not. The advantage of arbitrating first is to avoid the mediation quandary over how much to reveal and when to reveal it. Arbitration is relatively straightforward, like a trial. It is mediation where issues of what to reveal and how things might be construed become issues. But where the case has already been heard, most of those issues are erased. The parties also will have some sense of how well they performed in the arbitration. That knowledge helps them decide how to approach the mediation.

Medaloa and Baseball Arbitration

Medaloa and similar approaches are attempts to simplify the arbitration process and to control the outcome to the extent possible. Medaloa stands for *mediation and last offer arbitration*. In Medaloa, the dispute is mediated. If the parties reach an impasse, their last offers are presented to the mediator, who chooses one. That decision becomes binding, just like in arbitration. Similarly, in baseball arbitration, the arbitrator is presented with two options—the player's request and the team's proposal. These proposals come only after lengthy negotiations. The arbitrator chooses one, and the parties are bound.

In summary, flexibility is the critical element that makes arbitration a viable alternative to litigation. Parties can take the basic arbitration premise—choose a neutral to make a binding decision—and create a process that meets their needs. As long as the parties agree and none of their actions are illegal, they can agree to almost anything—no discovery or briefs, abbreviated hearings or even presentation of evidence on paper or over the internet. On the other hand, parties can agree to full-blown discovery, applying the rules of evidence, briefs, sequestered witnesses, and complete hearings with court reporters. Courts will not question the parties' agreement unless it appears that they did not freely give up the rights guaranteed by due process. Issues arise as to whether such waivers are voluntary when confronted by pre-dispute arbitration clauses entered into between the parties of unequal bargaining power. These issues will be discussed in the following chapter.

MANAGING COMPLEX ARBITRATIONS

In complex cases, arbitration can become more of a nightmare than a help. Too much discovery, too many witnesses, and too many documents make it nearly impossible to schedule and complete the arbitration. Historically, big arbitrations have been scheduled over time—that is, a day or two here and there as it fits into everyone's schedule. Many such arbitrations have taken over a year to complete. This scheduling disaster would never happen in court. It leads to fragmented trials and difficulty keeping track of all the details. Fortunately, there has been a move to expedite these cases so that the benefits of arbitration are once again obtained.

Allen Poppleton has set out a method for expediting complex cases which simplifies and clarifies matters that often create conflict in arbitration. He suggests that arbitrators should manage the proceedings with a firm hand, rather than passively, setting a schedule and keeping to it. The basic method he suggests is:

- A procedural conference is held in order to set ground rules;
- A discovery schedule should be devised;
- Cooperation will be required on exchanging information;
- Documents will be considered self-authenticating (subject to challenge);
- Depositions and affidavits will be encouraged, subject to the opponent's right to introduce other parts of the depositions and to cross-examine witnesses in person;
- Written biographies of witnesses will be introduced to avoid lengthy questioning;

- Charts, graphs, and summaries will be encouraged when presenting voluminous data;
- Lists of probable witnesses will be exchanged, as well as documents intended to be introduced;
- Briefs will be expected in advance of the hearing;
- Post-hearing briefs may be encouraged as a way to minimize testimony;
- The hearing itself will be expedited as well;
- Repetitive or argumentative cross-examination will be prohibited;
- Background information will be eliminated;
- Time need not be spent educating the arbitrator;
- Long days will help reduce arbitration days and encourage efficiency;
- Parties will be allotted a specific number of hearing days and expected to fit their case in that time (although additional time will be allotted if it becomes necessary); and
- The arbitrator will limit her own questions to clarifying ones.

Poppleton has used this approach successfully to expedite a complex case.[63]

---

63. Poppleton, Allen, "The Arbitrator's Role in Expediting the Large and Complex Commercial Case," *Arbitration Journal*, Volume 36, Number 4 (December 1981).

CHAPTER FOURTEEN:
CONTRACT CLAUSES REQUIRING ALTERNATIVE DISPUTE RESOLUTION

ADVANTAGES OF PRE-DISPUTE ADR CLAUSES

Agreeing to use ADR is a simple matter of contract. There are many ways to contract to use ADR. Parties may simply sign an Agreement to Mediate or Arbitrate after they are involved in a dispute. Appendix A sets out a standard Agreement to Mediate, and appendix F includes some examples of Agreements to Arbitrate used by companies that provide ADR services.

If they wish, parties to any kind of contract can incorporate a clause that provides for ways to handle disputes that arise during, or as a result of the execution of, the agreement. These clauses may be quite simple, setting out only what form of ADR will be used and specifying which provider's rules will apply. Or they can be quite complex, setting out a progression of steps to be followed when a dispute arises; for example, negotiation, then mediation, then arbitration. Arbitration agreements may be the most complex. They may specify which state law to apply, who the arbitrator will be or how the arbitrator will be chosen, what remedies are available, how discovery will be conducted, and numerous other provisions anticipating every conceivable issue that might arise. The idea behind including so many details in these agreements before a dispute is at hand is that it is best to take care of these issues while the parties are getting along rather than after they are unhappy with each other. Samples of several pre-dispute ADR clauses are included in appendix G.

ENFORCING PRE-DISPUTE CLAUSES

Questions about whether agreements to use ADR should be enforced are evaluated using principles of contract law. Is there mutual agreement? Are the terms clear? Parties who agree to use ADR after a dispute arises know their options and issues, and can enter into an agreement to use ADR with full knowledge of the rights they are waiving and the likely impact on the outcome of the dispute. Those who sign pre-dispute ADR clauses do not have the advantage of knowing what the issues will be and the problems likely to arise in addressing them. Like other contracts, however, courts usually uphold these future-looking agreements unless basic contract interpretation requires invalidation. The Eleventh Circuit Court of Appeals has endorsed "the strong federal policy favoring arbitration . . .[despite] hardships which arbitration brings for litigants, i.e., lack of discovery, evidentiary rules, jury and meaningful right to further review."[64] Therefore, understanding what you are agreeing to when signing a pre-dispute ADR clause is important.

Simple contract law is not *always* enough when the parties agree to use ADR in anticipation of possible future disputes. Pre-dispute ADR clauses are being used more often and in numerous types of agreements. They have long been used in construction agreements, where the parties expect disputes and want them resolved quickly and expertly. Increasingly, companies are requiring employees to sign agreements to arbitrate any disputes arising out of their employment. Consumers are signing arbitration clauses when they open stock or bank accounts, when they buy expensive items, or when they take out a loan. The clauses are inserted by the large corporation, rarely explained to the consumer, and usually do not provide for the protections afforded by our court system or by the Constitution. Often the clauses are inserted in multipage form agreements, such as those that we receive when we get a new credit card. They are not explained or even highlighted, so the average consumer does not understand the import of the clause. Courts have started reviewing these clauses to be sure that people are not being coerced into signing away their rights unknowingly or without ensuring sufficient protection for their due process rights.

---

64. *Paladino v. Avnet Computer Technologies, Inc.* 134 F.3d 1054, 1062 (C.A. 11th Cir. 1998).

Some of the issues that arise in debating the enforceability and effectiveness of pre-dispute ADR clauses are:

- Was the agreement made knowingly and voluntarily?
- Who bears the cost?
- What provisions have been made for ensuring a fair exchange of information?
- How are the neutrals chosen?
- Do the neutrals have any biases?
- Is the outcome binding?
- What awards and protections are allowed or required?

Gilmer v. Interstate/Johnson Lane Corporation is the seminal case in this area, upholding an employer's right to require employees to submit all claims arising out of employment to arbitration. In *Gilmer*, the Supreme Court held that, "even claims arising under a statute designed to further important social policies may be arbitrated because, 'So long as the prospective litigant effectively may vindicate [his or her] statutory cause of action in the arbitral forum,' the statute serves its functions."[65] Since then, many employers have required all disputes, including discrimination and harassment claims, to be arbitrated.[66]

More recently, the Supreme Court clarified the FAA even further in *Circuit City Stores v. Adams*, 121 S.Ct. 1399 (March 21, 2001). In that case, the Supreme Court narrowed the interpretation of section 1 of the FAA, which exempts workers engaged in interstate commerce from arbitration agreements. Since most business today is conducted through interstate commerce, the

---

65. *Id.* at 28, 111 S.Ct. 1647 (quoting *Mitsubishi, supra,* at p. 637, 105 S.Ct. 3346).

66. Richard A. Bales, "Creating and Challenging Compulsory Arbitration Agreements," 13 Lab. Law 511 (winter/spring 1998); Katherine Eddy, "To Every Remedy a Wrong: The Confounding of Civil Litigation Through Mandatory Arbitration Clauses in Employment Contracts," 52 Hastings L.J. 771 (Mar. 2001)

Court could easily have held that most employees were "engaged in interstate commerce." Instead, it held that only those directly involved in the transportation industry were exempted.[67] Therefore, most arbitration agreements in an employment contract will be upheld.

These cases have raised numerous issues about protections provided by arbitration, how to determine whether the parties were waiving their rights knowingly, and what remedies should be available in arbitration. Unrepresented parties signing a loan agreement rarely understand that, by signing an arbitration agreement, they are waiving their right to a trial by jury and most rights to appeal an unwanted verdict, as well as limiting their right to discovery in preparation for the hearing. Because of problems with these clauses, some courts have turned from almost a blanket refusal to review any disputes sent to arbitration to a much closer review and willingness to overturn arbitration decisions or to invalidate arbitration agreements.

From that early 1900s stance of invalidating arbitration clauses for usurping the role of the courts to the complete change to encouraging ADR, the courts have stepped back and are taking a closer look at arbitration agreements. While the grounds for invalidating contract clauses are becoming clearer, there still remain outstanding issues, and agreements must be examined individually.

---

67. In a case closely following *Circuit City, Perez v. Globe Airport Securities*, No. 0013489, 11th Cir. June 12, 2001, the eleventh circuit avoided the issue of whether an airport worker was "involved in interstate commerce."

INVALIDATING PRE-DISPUTE CLAUSES

Grounds on which pre-dispute clauses may be invalidated include:

- Making the process so expensive that it prohibits the putative plaintiff from pursuing his rights;[68]
- Not allowing sufficient discovery;[69]
- Limiting awards allowed so that parties cannot recover as completely as they could in court;[70] and
- Not clarifying in the original agreement that the issue now at hand is one that would be decided by the arbitrator.[71]

The issue faced by the courts is whether the arbitration agreement provides the parties with the same benefits and protections

---

68. *Green Tree Financial Corp.-Alabama v. Randolph*, 121 S.Ct. 513, 522 (2000) overturned an eleventh circuit decision invalidating a clause that did not specify who would pay costs. The Supreme Court found that the plaintiff did not show that the costs were so prohibitive that justice could not be served in arbitration, but did not preclude the possibility of such a finding. *But see Perez v. Globe Airport Securities*, No. 0013489, 11th Cir. June 12, 2001, in which the eleventh circuit held that an arbitration clause was unenforceable because it stated that the parties would split the cost, whereas Title VII, under which the claim was raised, allowed the decision-maker to award costs to the prevailing party. Therefore, the Court held, the agreement limited available remedies and was not enforceable. *See also Cole v. Burns Intern. Sec. Svcs.*, 105 F.3d 1465, 1481 (C.A.D.C. 1997), suggesting that costs to employees in mandatory arbitration clauses for employment disputes be reasonable and that the employer pay the arbitrator's costs.

69. *Pony Express Courier Corp. v. Morris*, 921 S.W.2d 817, 822 (Tx. App. 1996).

70. *Duffield v. Robertson Stephens & Co.*, 144 F.3d 1182 (9th Cir. 1998). *See also* Shelly Smith, "Mandatory Arbitration Clauses in Consumer Contracts: Consumer Protection and the Circumvention of the Judicial System," 50 DePaul L. Rev. 1191, 1234 (summer 2001).

71. *Paladino v. Avnet Computer Technologies, Inc.*, 134 F.3d 1054, 1060 (C.A.11 (Fla.), 1998.

as the court does.[72] The courts have begun reviewing the agreements in recent years because these clauses, especially the ones used in employment and consumer agreements, are not really arms-length transactions. As much as we can argue that an employee could go find another job, and therefore is not forced to sign this agreement, few employees would turn down a good job because of the arbitration clause, or even really understand what it is they are being asked to sign. The drafters of these agreements often are using the arbitration agreements to limit access to the court system, thus saving themselves money and effort by limiting the rights of their employees and customers. The circumstances are worlds apart from the pre-dispute clauses included in construction agreements, negotiated heavily by sophisticated attorneys for both sides.

Even with these concerns, courts generally uphold pre-dispute clauses except where there is a clear showing of prejudice to a party's rights. The Eleventh Circuit Court of Appeals held that requiring parties to pay arbitrator's fees may deny them access to justice because they would not have to pay the courts for the same service (aside from the minor filing fee).[73] But the Supreme Court overturned the ruling, stating that, absent a clear showing that the fees would be so expensive that they would preclude the plaintiff from vindicating his rights, a clause that does not specify who will pay costs is not unenforceable.[74] The fourth circuit held, however, that the courts will look to whether arbitration will cost significantly more than litigation that it would deter the bringing of claims.[75]

---

72. *See* Smith, *supra*, note 70.

73. *Green Tree*, 121 S.Ct. 513, 517.

74. *Id.*

75. *Bradford v. Rockwell Semiconductor Systems*, 238 F.3d 549 (4th Cir. 2001).

One of the issues the courts face in deciding whether cost provisions invalidate arbitration clauses is whether only the clause becomes invalid or whether the whole arbitration agreement is invalid because of the clause. In *Perez v. Globe Security Services, Inc.*, (No. 00-13489, 11th Cir. June 12, 2001), the eleventh circuit invalidated the entire agreement because to do otherwise would encourage the employer to include offending clauses until it was caught. *But see Gannon v. Circuit City Stores, Inc.*, (No. 00-3243, 8th Cir. August 17, 2001), in which the unenforceable cap on punitive damages was struck down but the agreement itself was upheld.

Another example of ways companies are using clauses to discourage litigation is requiring parties to waive the right to attorney representation during the agreed-upon arbitration. This waiver may be fair to a corporation that employs sophisticated claims adjusters or business people who are familiar with trials and arbitrations. But it is inherently unfair to a consumer with no legal expertise, who would have the right to representation in court.

Unfairness and unconscionability are clear bases for invalidating agreements. There have been many cases where the courts applied the doctrine of unconscionability to invalidate one-sided agreements, but the *Hooters* case is one of the best examples.[76] In that case, the employer wrote the agreement that was clearly one-sided. For example, the employee had to provide the employer with a specific statement of her claims, but the employer did not have to respond. The employer created the list of arbitrators from which the parties had to choose a panel. Also, Hooters allowed itself, but not the employee, to move for summary judgment or to include other matters in the claim. To make it more clearly unconscionable, Hooters allowed itself the right to modify the rules governing the arbitration or to cancel the Agreement to Arbitrate. The fourth circuit had little trouble

---

76. *Hooters of America, Inc. v. Phillips*, 173 F.3d 933 (4ᵗʰ Cir. 1999).

finding that the agreement created "a stacked deck" and that it was unenforceable.[77]

Some courts have examined agreements to determine whether the waiver of statutory rights, especially in discrimination cases, is knowing and voluntary. The ninth circuit has held that the individual must have exercised a "real choice" in selecting arbitration over litigation.[78] Other courts disagree, even those in California, and have held that ADR or arbitration clauses are interpreted just like any other contract—unless revocable on contract law grounds, the agreement is enforced.

In addition, where discovery is prohibited by the agreement or limited severely, the courts generally will not invalidate the agreement.[79] Since discovery is available by agreement of the parties, where they waive that right in their agreement, they "trade the procedures and opportunity for review of the courtroom for the simplicity, informality, and expedition of arbitration."[80] In the court system, of course, adequate discovery is allowed. Generally, prohibiting discovery benefits the defendant, who holds all the cards. Defendant has all corporate records, access to all witnesses still employed, and the power to persuade witnesses to see the dispute from the corporate viewpoint.

There is also an issue as to the neutrality of the arbitrators. When large corporations are involved in numerous arbitrations, they use the same arbitrators time and again. Understandably, there is concern that these arbitrators cannot

---

77. 173 F.3d at p. 940. *See also Arnold v. United Companies Lending Co.*, 511 S.E. 2d 854 (W.Va. 1998); *Iwen v. U.S. West District*, 977 P.2d 989 (Mont. 1999).

78. *Duffield*, at p. 1199. *See also Lawrence v. Walzer & Gabrielson*, 256 Cal. Rptr. 6, 9 (Cal. App. 2d Dist. 1989).

79. *Gilmer*, at p. 31; *Pony Express* at p. 822 (an arbitration clause that prohibits discovery is not unconscionable on its face).

80. *Gilmer*, at p. 31, quoting *Mitsubishi*, *supra* note 60, at p. 628.

possibly remain unbiased—if not from the obvious issue of frequent paychecks, then more subtly from getting to know the attorneys and representatives for the corporation. Additionally, the lack of reasoned decision in most arbitrations makes review for bias nearly impossible.

One of the biggest issues in invalidating arbitration agreements is limiting remedies the arbitrator can award. Of course any putative defendant would want to limit damages that could be awarded against him. But if placing such limits restricts the possible recovery, access to justice is in question. The California Supreme Court has held that an arbitrator must have the power to order the same remedies available to a judge under state law.[80] The eleventh circuit in *Paladino* held that "the arbitration agreement's terms regarding remedies must also be fully consistent with the purposes underlying any statutory claims subject to arbitration, quoting *Gilmer*, which stated that "[b]y agreeing to arbitrate a statutory claim, a party does not forego the substantive rights afforded by the statute; it only submits to their resolution in an arbitral, rather than a judicial, forum."[81] The first thing the courts do is look to see what the state laws allow. There are some state laws that limit the remedies available. One question is whether such laws apply in arbitration. If state law allows a remedy in question, the courts look to the agreement to see if the parties have prohibited it. Such a decision may be upheld in a post-dispute agreement, but again, not necessarily upheld in a pre-dispute agreement.

Finally, the issue of arbitrability is important. Arbitrability is the question of whether a specific issue or dispute is to be decided by the arbitrator or must be taken to court. Some arbitration agreements specify that only issues arising out of interpretation of the

---

80. *Armendariz v. Foundation Health Psychare Services, Inc.* 24 Cal. 4th 83 (Sup. Ct. Cal. 2000).

81. *Gilmer*, quoting *Mitsubishi Motors Corp. v. Soler Chrysler-Plymouth, Inc.* See also *Perez v. Globe Airport Securities*, No. 0013489, 11th Cir. June 12, 2001, discussed *supra* at note 68.

contract may be decided by the arbitrator. If someone raises an issue of discrimination, then, arguably, it is not "arbitrable." Instead, it is a question for the court. Problems arise, however, when clauses are vague. If a buy/sell agreement specifies "all issues arising out of this agreement," does it include the *next* shipment? Does it include tort claims (injuries from a fistfight between the delivery person and the receiving clerk)? Generally, the court decides whether those issues should be arbitrated unless the arbitration agreement provides otherwise.[83] Where the clause is unclear, the courts generally hold that it cannot be interpreted to contravene state law. For example, in *Paladino* the eleventh circuit held that a clause that allowed an arbitrator to award damages only for breach of contract could not be applied to require arbitration of Title VII claims. If the arbitrator could not make an award on such claims, he could not arbitrate them, the Court held.

A more general complaint about pre-dispute clauses is that they allow corporations or even governments to use arbitration to hide issues that affect the public. Because no written opinions are published, no precedent is set. Important issues may be decided by a single arbitrator which can have a resounding effect, with no requirement even of a simple reason for the decision. For example, in *Jeremiah J. O'Keefe, Sr., et. al. v. Loewen Group, Inc., et. al*, No. 91677-423 (Cir. Ct. 1ˢᵗ Jud. Dist. Miss. (1995), a Canadian company lost a commercial lawsuit in Mississippi. It then filed a claim under NAFTA (North American Free Trade Agreement) seeking reimbursement on the grounds that the jury was biased against Canadians. While the jury decision received plenty of media attention, the arbitration was kept secret under the applicable World Bank rules.

---

83. *First Options of Chicago, Inc. v. Kaplan*, 115 S.Ct. 1920, 1924 (1995) (who decides arbitrability of claims depends on what the parties agreed to. If the parties did not agree that the arbitrators will decide such issues, then the court should decide the question "just as it would decide any other question that the parties did not submit to arbitration . . .").

DRAFTING PRE-DISPUTE CLAUSES

Despite increased court review, pre-dispute ADR clauses may be useful in many arenas. Careful thought and drafting can avoid issues that have proved problematic for others. The first issue that should be considered in drafting these clauses is which processes to include. Some considerations are:

- What types of disputes are likely to arise?
- Is there an ongoing relationship?
- How quickly do the likely disputes need to be decided?
- Will there be issues of precedent?

Generally, a multistep approach is best when complex disputes are likely. First, negotiation may be required. Depending upon the types of disputes, the parties might want to set forth provisions now, while the parties are getting along, on how to structure a negotiation—where, when, who will be present, etc.

If negotiations fail, many complex clauses require mediation. Again, formalities may be decided in advance, even to the point of naming the mediator. While such agreements often feel like prenuptial agreements (Why would we want to have such an agreement? We're in love and will never, ever fight!), experience teaches us that it is better to think about the harsh realities now rather than later when we are feeling much less charitable.

Finally, most ADR agreements end with binding arbitration. Others send claims to litigation if mediation is unsuccessful. Clauses can be very simple, such as the first one included in appendix G. Parties may merely agree to arbitration and choose the rules to apply ("to be conducted under the rules of Resolution Resources"). On the other hand, clauses can be extremely complex, on the assumption that there will be disputes. Only the most complex transactions usually require complex clauses.

In drafting an arbitration clause, these are some of the factors to consider:

- What kind of disputes the arbitration agreement should include:
    - All disputes arising under the agreement;
    - Disputes relating to only a portion of the project;
    - All disputes except claims of discrimination or other civil rights violations;
    - Tort claims, statutory claims, or just those relating to or requiring interpretation of the original contract;
- Forum—the location for the hearing:
    - What state laws to apply;
    - Whether the FAA applies; and
    - Specific discovery provisions;
- How disputes about discovery or other prehearing matters will be handled;
- Who will decide threshold issues of arbitrability? Court or arbitrator (if not specified, the court decides);
- What rules to apply—AAA, RRC, CPR, or your modification;
- Timing—hearing, discovery, motions, payment, or performance;
- How to choose the arbitrator(s), and what happens if one party fails to choose in a timely manner;
- Remedies allowed, including punitive damages, attorneys fees, specific performance, interest, and costs;
- Who will pay the costs of arbitration;
- Who will pay attorneys fees;
- What rules of evidence, if any, apply;
- Whether a reasoned decision will be required; and
- Anything specific to your dispute that will affect or modify the way the arbitration will be conducted most effectively.

Several sample clauses are included in appendix G.[84] They may be used as they are or modified to meet the specific needs of each agreement. Note that few of them discuss all or even most of these issues. Simple is usually better, with the understanding that an experienced ADR provider can help you work out the details if and when necessary.

Arbitration Clauses in Employment Agreements

As discussed earlier, the courts have been pretty strict in enforcing arbitration clauses in an employment context. They want to ensure that everyone is protected in pursuing their claims. The EEOC has taken the position that a mandatory arbitration provision that is required as a condition of employment is inconsistent with the civil rights statutes enforced by the EEOC.[85] In *EEOC v. Luce, Forward, Hamilton & Scripps*,[86] the California court held that an employer violated Title VII by discharging an employee for refusing to sign an Agreement to Arbitrate Title VII cases.

---

84. In addition to the attached samples, there are other sources for samples, including numerous articles on the World Wide Web. In 1997 AAA created a booklet detailing considerations in drafting clauses for a variety of types of agreements. It includes numerous samples as well as explanations. That booklet can be obtained from AAA.

85. Policy Statement on Mandatory Binding Arbitration of Employment Discrimination Disputes as a Condition of Employment (1997).

86. 2 F.Supp.2d 1080 (C.D. Calif. 2000) Issues surrounding arbitration clauses in the employment context are discussed more fully in *After Circuit City—Arbitration of Individual Employment Disputes*, by Ross Runkel, Director of the National Arbitration Center, and is available on the Web at http://www.lawmemo.com/emp/articles/circuitcity.htm.

Cole v. Burns International. Security Services[87] interpreted *Gilmer* as requiring five safeguards when an employer, as a condition of employment, requires arbitration of future disputes involving federal statutes: (1) a neutral arbitrator, (2) more than minimal discovery, (3) a written award, (4) availability of all remedies that would be available in court, and (5) no requirement for the employee to pay *either* unreasonable costs or any of the arbitrator's fees or expenses. The move toward having the employer pay for the arbitration can be a considerable expense, and employers should stop and think about whether they want to have a blanket arbitration requirement.

To complicate matters further, however, employers who wish to have their employees sign arbitration clauses have to consider how the clause will affect the employee's employment status. Most states are "employment-at-will" states, meaning that employees can be fired for any reason or no reason at all, as long as the action is not discriminatory. Where employers make arbitration a condition or term of employment, a question arises as to whether the employee's status changes and an employment agreement is implied. If so, the employer faces questions of whether due process rights were provided in the termination.[88] For this reason, many employers are creating separate agreements, stating specifically that they are not employment agreements. Some, on the other hand, are using the creation of rights in employment as an incentive to get employees to sign arbitration agreements.

---

87. *Cole v. Burns Intern. Sec. Svcs.*, 105 F.3d 1465, 1481 (C.A.D.C. 1997). *See also Bales* at 530–31; *McCaskill v. SCI Management Corp.*, 2000 WL 875396 (N.D. Ill. 2000), finding that, given the arbitrator's liberal discretion to grant an award, the fact that the arbitration agreement required the employee to pay her own costs and attorneys fees did not preclude her subsequent recovery.

88. *Swanson v. Liquid Air Corp.*, 826 P.2d 664, 668 (Wash. 1992); *Perling v. Citizens and Southern Nat'l Bank*, 300 S.E.2d 649, 652 (Ga. 1983); *See also Bales, supra* note 89 at pp. 523–525.

To summarize, ADR clauses may be a useful tool but careful consideration needs to be given to all the parties. Due process must be protected. The purpose of ADR is to provide fair, reasonable, inexpensive, and quick resolutions. Clauses should be drafted with these goals in mind.

APPENDIX A

AGREEMENT TO MEDIATE[89]

Case Style Here

This is an agreement between   and   ,
(hereinafter referred to as "the parties"), their representatives
and Resolution Resources Corporation (RRC), represented
by   . The Parties have agreed to enter into mediation
with RRC with the intention of reaching a consensual settlement of their dispute.

1. The parties and their representatives understand that the
purpose of the mediation is to attempt to find a mutually acceptable resolution of the dispute through cooperative attempts to
solve the problems which presently separate them. To achieve a
mutually acceptable resolution, the mediator, the parties and
their counsel will work to ensure that each party understands the
facts asserted and the contentions of all parties.

2. In order for the mediation to be successful, open and honest
communications are essential. Accordingly, the parties are
urged to make complete and accurate disclosure of all matters
relevant to the process of settlement.

3. All communications by the parties shall be treated as strictly
confidential by the mediator, by the parties and by their representatives. The mediator will not disclose any information
learned during the mediation without the express permission of
the parties. Confidential matters disclosed in a private meeting
or caucus with one party will not be divulged to the other party
without the consent of the party making the disclosure.

4. In order to maintain confidentiality, the parties and their
representatives, by this agreement, agree not to call the mediator

---

89. Resolution Resources Corporation

as a witness at any proceeding nor to subpoena or otherwise seek discovery of any written materials in his/her possession developed for or in the course of this mediation. To the extent that the law permits such discovery from the mediator, the parties hereby waive their rights thereto.

5. The exception to the confidentiality rules stated in paragraphs 3 and 4 is that this agreement to mediate and any written agreement made and signed by the parties as a result of the mediation may be used in any relevant proceeding, unless the parties, by written agreement, decide otherwise.

6. Nothing in this agreement shall be construed to prevent or excuse the mediator from reporting matters such as crimes, imminent threats of bodily injury to a child or a party, or such other matters as to which the law imposes a duty to report.

7. It is expressly understood by the parties and their representatives that the mediator does not offer legal advice in this mediation and is not functioning as an attorney whether or not the mediator is in fact an attorney. In this mediation, the mediator's role is to aid the parties in seeking a fair agreement in accordance with their respective interests. The construction of a proposed agreement and any question of law should be referred by the parties to their own legal counsel.

8. The mediator will not represent any party or any participant in this mediation in any subsequent legal proceeding or matter relating to the subject of the mediation.

9. RRC recommends that each party be represented by counsel to whom all questions of law should be addressed. RRC will work with counsel for the parties throughout the mediation to help facilitate an agreement.

10. Mediation is a voluntary, non-binding process. The mediation may be terminated by either party at any time. The parties, however, agree that the subject of termination is a proper one for discussion at the mediation. The mediator may terminate the mediation in the event he/she finds that one of the parties is not

acting in good faith, or if it is felt that further negotiations would not be productive.

11. The parties agree to share the fee of RRC. The fee in this mediation is $___ per party per hour or part thereof of mediation time including preparation and pre-session discussions with the parties or their counsel. The administrative fee will be $100.00 per party. The administrative fee is payable prior to the execution of this agreement. All other fees are payable at the close of each mediation session. The attorneys whose signatures appear below are primarily responsible for the payment of the fees in this proceeding.

12. Neither RRC nor any mediator shall be liable to any party for any act or omission in connection with any mediation conducted under this Agreement.

I have read, understand and agree to each of the provisions of this agreement.

_____   _____

_____   _____

_____   _____

For Resolution Resources Corporation:

_____   _____

Any intern/observer whose attendance is permitted by the parties will hold all matters heard or observed in complete confidence.

_____

APPENDIX B

OPENING STATEMENT CHECKLIST[90]

1. Introduce yourself.

2. Commend the parties on their willingness to participate in mediation.

3. Explain the concept of voluntariness.

4. Explain the role of the mediator.

   - Impartial/neutral; and
   - Facilitator/not legal or financial advisor.

5. Explain the role of the parties and attorneys as problem solvers.

6. Explain the mediation process.

   - Opening Statements by the parties;
   - Joint Session;
   - Caucus;
   - Confidentiality, both in process and in caucus;
   - Reconvening the joint session;
   - Writing the agreement; and
   - Note taking by the mediator (all notes destroyed at conclusion of mediation).

7. Ask for questions from the parties or attorneys.

8. Get a joint commitment to begin.

---

90. Created and reprinted with permission by Beverly K. Schaffer, Ph.D., Director of the Violence Studies Program at Emory University.

APPENDIX C

MODEL STANDARDS OF CONDUCT
FOR MEDIATORS[91]

The Model Standards of Conduct for Mediators were prepared from 1992 through 1994 by a joint committee composed of two delegates from the American Arbitration Association, John D. Feerick, Chair, and David Botwinik, two from the American Bar Association, James Alfini and Nancy Rogers, and two from the Society of Professionals in Dispute Resolution, Susan Dearborn and Lemoine Pierce.

The Model Standards have been approved by the American Arbitration Association, the Litigation Section and the Dispute Resolution Section of the American Bar Association, and the Society of Professionals in Dispute Resolution.

Reporters: Bryant Garth and Kimberlee K. Kovach

Staff Project Director: Frederick E. Woods

The views set out in this publication have not been considered by the American Bar Association House of Delegates and do not constitute the policy of the American Bar Association.

Introductory Note

The initiative for these standards came from three professional groups: The American Arbitration Association, the American Bar Association, and the Society of Professionals in Dispute Resolution.

---

91. ©2002. Reprinted with permission of the American Arbitration Association and the American Bar Association.

I. Self-Determination: A Mediator shall Recognize that Mediation is Based on the Principle of Self-Determination by the Parties.

Self-determination is the fundamental principle of mediation. It requires that the mediation process rely upon the ability of the parties to reach a voluntary, uncoerced agreement. Any party may withdraw from mediation at any time.

Comments

- The mediator may provide information about the process, raise issues, and help parties explore options. The primary role of the mediator is to facilitate a voluntary resolution of a dispute. Parties shall be given the opportunity to consider all proposed options.

- A mediator cannot personally ensure that each party has made a fully informed choice to reach a particular agreement, but is a good practice for the mediator to make the parties aware of the importance of consulting other professionals, where appropriate, to help them make informed decisions.

II. Impartiality: A Mediator shall Conduct the Mediation in an Impartial Manner.

The concept of mediator impartiality is central to the mediation process. A mediator shall mediate only those matters in which she or he can remain impartial and evenhanded. If at any time the mediator is unable to conduct the process in an impartial manner, the mediator is obligated to withdraw.

Comments

- A mediator shall avoid conduct that gives the appearance of partiality toward one of the parties. The quality of the mediation process is enhanced when the parties have confidence in the impartiality of the mediator.

- When mediators are appointed by a court or institution, the appointing agency shall make reasonable efforts to ensure that mediators serve impartially.

- A mediator should guard against partiality or prejudice based on the parties' personal characteristics, background or performance at the mediation.

III. Conflicts of Interest: A Mediator shall Disclose all Actual and Potential Conflicts of Interest Reasonably Known to the Mediator. After Disclosure, the Mediator shall Decline to Mediate unless all Parties Choose to Retain the Mediator. The Need to Protect Against Conflicts of Interest also Governs Conduct that Occurs During and After the Mediation.

A conflict of interest is a dealing or relationship that might create an impression of possible bias. The basic approach to questions of conflict of interest is consistent with the concept of self-determination. The mediator has a responsibility to disclose all actual and potential conflicts that are reasonably known to the mediator and could reasonably be seen as raising a question about impartiality. If all parties agree to mediate after being informed of conflicts, the mediator may proceed with the mediation. If, however, the conflict of interest casts serious doubt on the integrity of the process, the mediator shall decline to proceed.

A mediator must avoid the appearance of conflict of interest both during and after the mediation. Without the consent of all parties, a mediator shall not subsequently establish a professional relationship with one of the parties in a related matter, or in an unrelated matter under circumstances which would raise legitimate questions about the integrity of the mediation process.

Comments

- A mediator shall avoid conflicts of interest in recommending the services of other professionals. A mediator may make reference to professional referral services or associations which maintain rosters of qualified professionals.

- Potential conflicts of interest may arise between administrators of mediation programs and mediators and there may be strong pressures on the mediator to settle a particular case or cases. The mediator's commitment must be to the parties and the process. Pressure from outside of the mediation process should never influence the mediator to coerce parties to settle.

IV. Competence: A Mediator shall Mediate Only When the Mediator has the Necessary Qualifications to Satisfy the Reasonable Expectations of the Parties.

Any person may be selected as a mediator, provided that the parties are satisfied with the mediator's qualifications. Training and experience in mediation, however, are often necessary for effective mediation. A person who offers herself or himself as available to serve as a mediator gives parties and the public the expectation that she or he has the competency to mediate effectively. In court-connected or other forms of mandated mediation, it is essential that mediators assigned to the parties have the requisite training and experience.

Comments

- Mediators should have information available for the parties regarding their relevant training, education and experience.

- The requirements for appearing on the list of mediators must be made public and available to interested persons.

- When mediators are appointed by a court or institution, the appointing agency shall make reasonable efforts to ensure that each mediator is qualified for the particular mediation.

V. Confidentiality: A Mediator shall Maintain the Reasonable Expectations of the Parties with Regard to Confidentiality.

The reasonable expectations of the parties with regard to confidentiality shall be met by the mediator. The parties' expectations of confidentiality depend on the circumstances of the mediation and any agreements they may make. The mediator shall not disclose any matter that a party expects to be confidential unless given permission by all parties or unless required by law or other public policy.

Comments

- The parties may make their own rules with respect to confidentiality, or other accepted practice of an individual mediator or institution may dictate a particular set of expectations. Since the parties' expectations regarding confidentiality are important, the mediator should discuss these expectations with the parties.

- If the mediator holds private sessions with a party, the nature of these sessions with regard to confidentiality should be discussed prior to undertaking such sessions.

- In order to protect the integrity of the mediation, a mediator should avoid communicating information about how the parties acted in the mediation process, the merits of the case, or settlement offers. The mediator may report, if required, whether parties appeared at a scheduled mediation.

- Where the parties have agreed that all or a portion of the information disclosed during a mediation is confidential, the parties' agreement should be respected by the mediator.

- Confidentiality should not be construed to limit or prohibit the effective monitoring, research, or evaluation of mediation programs by responsible persons. Under appropriate circumstances, researchers may be permitted to obtain access to the statistical data and, with the permission of the parties, to individual case files, observations of live mediations, and interviews with participants.

VI. Quality of the Process: A Mediator shall Conduct the Mediation Fairly, Diligently, and in a Manner Consistent with the Principle of Self-Determination by the Parties.

A mediator shall work to ensure a quality process and to encourage mutual respect among the parties. A quality process requires a commitment by the mediator to diligence and procedural fairness. There should be adequate opportunity for each party in the mediation to participate in the discussions. The parties decide when and under what conditions they will reach an agreement or terminate a mediation.

Comments

- A mediator may agree to mediate only when he or she is prepared to commit the attention essential to an effective mediation.

- Mediators should only accept cases when they can satisfy the reasonable expectations of the parties concerning the timing of the process. A mediator should not allow a mediation to be unduly delayed by the parties or their representatives.

- The presence or absence of persons at a mediation depends on the agreement of the parties and the mediator. The parties and mediator may agree that others may be excluded from particular sessions or from the entire mediation process.

- The primary purpose of a mediator is to facilitate the parties' voluntary agreement. This role differs substantially from other professional-client relationships. Mixing the role of a mediator and the role of a professional advising a client is problematic, and mediators must strive to distinguish between the roles. A mediator should, therefore, refrain from providing professional advice. Where appropriate, a mediator should recommend that parties seek outside professional advice, or consider resolving their dispute through arbitration, counseling, neutral evaluation, or other processes. A mediator who undertakes, at the request of the parties, an additional dispute resolution role in the same matter assumes increased responsibilities and obligations that may be governed by the standards of other processes.

- A mediator shall withdraw from a mediation when incapable of serving or when unable to remain impartial.

- A mediator shall withdraw from a mediation or postpone a session if the mediation is being used to further illegal conduct, or if a party is unable to participate due to drug, alcohol, or other physical or mental incapacity.

- Mediators should not permit their behavior in the mediation process to be guided by a desire for a high settlement rate.

VII. Advertising and Solicitation: A Mediator shall be Truthful in Advertising and Solicitation for Mediation.

Advertising or any other communication with the public concerning services offered or regarding the education, training, and expertise of the mediator shall be truthful. Mediators shall refrain from promises and guarantees of results.

Comments

- It is imperative that communication with the public educate and instill confidence in the process.

- In an advertisement or other communication to the public, a mediator may make a reference to meeting state, national, or private organization qualifications only if the entity referred to has a procedure for qualifying mediators and the mediator has been duly granted the requisite status.

VIII. Fees: A Mediator shall fully Disclose and Explain the Basis of Compensation, Fees, and Charges to the Parties.

The parties should be provided sufficient information about fees at the outset of a mediation to determine if they wish to retain the services of a mediator. If a mediator charges fees, the fees shall be reasonable, considering among other things, the mediation service, the type and complexity of the matter, the expertise of the mediator, the time required, and the rates customary in the community. The better practice in reaching an understanding about fees is to set down the arrangements in a written agreement.

Comments

- A mediator who withdraws from a mediation should return any unearned fee to the parties.

- A mediator should not enter into a fee agreement which is contingent upon the result of the mediation or amount of the settlement.

- Co-mediators who share a fee should hold to standards of reasonableness in determining the allocation of fees. A mediator should not accept a fee for referral of a matter to another mediator or to any other person.

IX. Obligations to the Mediation Process: Mediators have a Duty to Improve the Practice of Mediation.

Comment

- Mediators are regarded as knowledgeable in the process of mediation. They have an obligation to use their knowledge to help educate the public about mediation; to make mediation accessible to those who would like to use it; to correct abuses; and to improve their professional skills and abilities. Copies of the Model Standards of Conduct for Mediators are available from the offices of the participating organizations.

APPENDIX D

COMMENTARY ON ETHICAL ISSUES BY THE GEORGIA OFFICE OF DISPUTE RESOLUTION[92]

IN JUNE, 1994, THE GEORGIA COMMISSION ON DISPUTE RESOLUTION TURNED ITS ATTENTION TO THE DEVELOPMENT OF A CODE OF ETHICAL BEHAVIOR FOR MEDIATORS SERVING COURT PROGRAMS IN GEORGIA. WE INITIATED A DIALOGUE WITH PRACTICING MEDIATORS IN THE STATE. THIS DIALOGUE SERVED AS THE STARTING POINT FOR THE DEVELOPMENT OF THE CODE.

THE CODE CONSISTS OF TWO PARTS. THE FIRST PART CONTAINS STANDARDS OF PRACTICE, THE FOUNDATION OF ETHICAL BEHAVIOR BY MEDIATORS. BECAUSE THE COMMISSION IS COGNIZANT OF THE LIMITED GUIDANCE PROVIDED THROUGH MERE ARTICULATION OF STANDARDS, COMMENTARY, INCLUDING SPECIFIC EXAMPLES FROM PRACTICE, ACCOMPANIES EACH STANDARD, ENHANCING AND STRENGTHENING THIS FOUNDATION.

SPECIFIC PRACTICE RULES, TREATING MATTERS OF CONDUCT WHICH ARE SETTLED AND DO NOT LEND THEMSELVES TO THE EXERCISE OF DISCRETION ON THE PART OF THE MEDIATOR, APPEAR AS PART V. RULES OF FAIR PRACTICE.

INTRODUCTION

The Georgia Commission on Dispute Resolution believes that ethical standards for mediators can be most easily understood in the context of the three fundamental promises that the mediator makes to the parties in explaining the process: 1) the mediator

---

92. Reprinted with permission by the Georgia Commission on Dispute Resolution.

will protect the self-determination of the parties; 2) the mediator will protect the confidentiality of the mediation process; 3) the mediator is a neutral who is impartial and is without bias or prejudice toward any party. Besides maintaining fidelity to these principles, a mediator acts as guardian of the overall fairness of the process.

I. SELF-DETERMINATION/VOLUNTARINESS:

Where the court orders that parties participate in a dispute resolution process other than trial, the process must be non-binding so as not to interfere with parties' constitutional right to trial. To that extent, all court-ordered ADR processes are voluntary. However, the self-determination of the parties which is a hallmark of mediation is of a different and far more subtle order.

Commentary: The Georgia Commission on Dispute Resolution accepts the proposition that self-determination of the parties is the most critical principle underlying the mediation process. Control of the outcome by the parties is the source of the power of the mediation process. Further, it is the characteristic which may lead to an outcome superior to an adjudicated outcome.

Self-determination is a difficult goal in our society in which people seem often unwilling to assume responsibility for their own lives, anxious for someone else to make the decisions for them. Mediation is antithetical to this attitude.

A. In order for parties to exercise self-determination they must understand the mediation process and be willing to participate in the process. A principal duty of the mediator is to fully explain the mediation process. This explanation should include:

1. An explanation of the role of the mediator as a neutral person who will facilitate the discussion between the parties but who will not coerce or control the outcome;

2. An explanation of the procedure which will be followed during the mediation session;

3. An explanation of the pledge of confidentiality which binds the mediator and any limitations upon the extent of confidentiality;

4. An explanation of the fact that the mediator will not give legal or financial advice and that if expert advice is needed, parties will be expected to refer to outside experts;

5. An explanation that where participation is mandated by the court, the participation of the parties is all that is required and settlement cannot be mandated;

6. An explanation that the mediation can be terminated at any time by the mediator or the parties;

7. An explanation that parties who participate in mediation are expected to negotiate in an atmosphere of good faith and full disclosure of matters material to any agreement reached;

8. An explanation that the parties are free to consult legal counsel at any time and are encouraged to have any agreement reviewed by independent counsel prior to signing;

9. An explanation that a mediated agreement, once signed, can have a significant effect upon the rights of the parties and upon the status of the case.

B. The mediator has an obligation to assure that every party has the capacity to participate in the mediation conference. Where an incapacity cannot be redressed, the mediation should be rescheduled or canceled.

Self-determination includes the ability to bargain for oneself alone or with the assistance of an attorney. Although the mediator has a duty to make every effort to address a power imbalance, this may be impossible. At some point the balance of power may be so skewed that the mediation should be terminated.

Commentary: Georgia mediators are confident of their ability to recognize serious incapacity. Situations in which there is a subtle incapacity are more troubling. Several mediators expressed concern about situations in which they questioned capacity to bargain but felt certain that the agreement in question would be in the best interest of the party and that going to court would be very traumatic. Should the mediation be terminated because of suspected incapacity if mediation is the gentler forum for a fragile person and the agreement which the other party is willing to make is favorable? Does the mediator's substituting his or her judgment for the judgment of the party destroy any possibility of self-determination? Is self-determination and the empowerment which it offers a rigid requirement in every mediation? Does it make a difference whether the suspected incapacity is temporary—i.e. a party is intoxicated—so that the mediation could be rescheduled?

__Example 1:__ The husband, who is a doctor, is also an alcoholic. The mediator notes, "She could have said anything and he would have said yes. He just wanted to get it over with. It was really hard keeping him there. I had to make two pots of coffee during each session to keep him going. He was just ready to get out and go get a drink or something." The wife is represented, but he is not represented. Both parties are concerned about preserving his assets, and they both agree that she should get a large portion of the assets. There seems to be danger that the assets will disappear because of his alcoholism. The mediator is concerned that the husband is agreeing too readily and is worried about the balance of power. The party is not presently incapacitated—except to the extent that his desire to complete the mediation is interfering with his giving careful thought to the process. It may be that the level of self-determination which he is exhibiting is the highest level that is possible for him. Should this person be deprived of the benefits which he might derive from mediation because he is not able to bargain as effectively as the other party?

__Example 2:__ During the mediation it becomes apparent to the mediator that one party is well represented and the other party is not being adequately represented. What, if anything, should the mediator do? If the mediator interferes in the attorney-client relationship a number of issues are raised. Would interference infringe upon the self-determination of the party who has retained the attorney? Is neutrality compromised? Is the mediator crossing a line and in effect *giving legal advice? If the mediator is compensated, will the mediator's action or inaction be influenced by the desire to maintain good relationships with attorneys for business reasons?*

Recommendation: Where a party is laboring under an incapacity which makes him or her incapable of effective bargaining, the mediator should terminate the mediation. Mediation is not an appropriate forum for the protection of the rights of a person who cannot bargain for him or herself.

If the incapacity is temporary—i.e. intoxication—the mediation should be rescheduled.

If there is a serious imbalance of power between parties, the mediator should consider whether the presence of an attorney, family member, or friend would give the needed support.

An obvious example of a power imbalance occurs when there is a history of domestic violence. Although the Commission has drawn up guidelines to assist court programs in identifying those cases which are not appropriate for mediation, information about a history of domestic violence may surface for the first time during the mediation. The questions the mediator faces are whether to terminate the mediation and, if so, how to safely terminate it. Factors which should be considered are whether there was more than one incident, when the incident or incidents occurred, whether the information surfaces during a joint session or during caucus, whether the alleged victim is intimidated. If the mediator has any concern that the safety of any person will be jeopardized by continuing the mediation, the mediation should be terminated.

If one party is simply unable to bargain as effectively as another, it is probably inappropriate to deny those parties the benefits of the mediation process because of that factor.

If the imbalance occurs because of disparity in the ability of the parties' attorneys, the principle of self-determination, in this case in relation to the selection of an attorney, again prevails.

One mediator expressed his view this way: "I am reluctant to withdraw where there is an imbalance in power because I always try to look at the alternative. The alternative usually is that person is going to be no better off in litigation. I understand that there's a judge there that can look after the parties, but still my practical experience in litigation teaches me that most parties are not going to be much better off in litigation rather than mediation if lack of power is their problem."

C. Parties cannot bargain effectively unless they have sufficient information. Informed consent to an agreement implies that parties not only knowingly agree to every term of the agreement but that they have had sufficient information to bargain effectively in reaching that agreement. Self-determination of the parties in a mediation includes not only informed consent to any agreement reached but participation in crafting the agreement as well.

Commentary: One mediator suggested that the parties who are operating without full information be asked to reconvene with attorneys present. This mediator said, "I have been more and more impressed with how effective a subsequent session can be with the attorneys present and everyone having prepared for it."

Example 1: One party says that there are assets which have been hidden and the other party denies the existence of the assets. The mediator faces the question of whether to push them forward on the facts that are established or give any credence to these alleged facts.

Recommendation: The question is resolved in favor of terminating or rescheduling the mediation if there has not been sufficient discovery or the party claiming that assets have been hidden feels that she or he cannot bargain effectively. The closer question comes if there is unsubstantiated suspicion—i.e. "He must have made more than he reported on his income taxes in 1992, so where is it?"

Domestic relations mediators who work in court-annexed or court-referred programs may not have the luxury of several sessions so that parties can be assigned "homework." As long as the information on assets and budgets is available, the actual preparation of lists of assets and liabilities and the preparation of budgets may provide an important opportunity for collaborative work by the parties.

Example 2: In a divorce mediation the wife is clearly dependent on the lawyer, as she had been on her husband while they were married. The lawyer is not cooperative in the mediation. At each session the lawyer comes in with a totally new agenda and without promised information. The mediator finds that she is spending an inordinate amount of time dealing with the lawyer. The mediator offers to meet with the parties alone, but the lawyers will not allow that.

Recommendation: *The mediator may caucus with the lawyers alone and confront the lawyer who is obstructing the mediation. The mediator may also raise questions in caucus with the lawyer and the client which may alert the client to the need to control the lawyer. Beyond this, it is difficult to resolve this situation without compromising the self-determination of the client or compromising neutrality.*

Commentary: Yet another variation on the issue of missing information is the missing issue—should the mediator bring up issues which the parties have not identified? As one mediator expressed this: "What's our role when people say we want you to mediate this case? Are we to mediate the issues that they bring to us or are we to create issues for them to discuss and decide about? I guess that a lot of the conflict that we're talking about here is what do we as mediators have to initiate or inform people or educate people about: all the issues that can be and probably ought to be discussed in the context of a divorce mediation? You're potentially opening up all these cans of worms for people who don't necessarily want them opened." On the other hand, have the parties had an opportunity to mediate from a position of full information if they have not considered every relevant issue? Beyond this, will the agreement hold up if it is not made in the context of all issues in the dispute?

D. The mediator must guard against any coercion of parties in obtaining a settlement.

Commentary: Many mediators discussed the question of when to declare impasse. One mediator said that she loved the point of impasse because the parties have "gone through the conflict" to get to impasse. She felt that the moment of impasse is a moment of great opportunity. At some point, however, persistence becomes coercion. The question of when to terminate the mediation will be discussed further under the topic of fairness.

E. It is improper for a lawyer/mediator, therapist/mediator, or mediator who has any professional expertise in another area to offer professional advice to a party. If the mediator feels that a party is acting without sufficient information, the mediator should raise the possibility of the party's consulting an expert to supply that information.

Commentary: Conversations with Georgia mediators who are trained as lawyers confirmed that this concept is extremely difficult for lawyer/mediators. Lawyers, having been trained to protect others, agonize over the perception that missing information, poor representation, ignorance of a defense, etc. may place a party in danger.

Recommendation: The line between information and advice can be very difficult to find. However, failure to honor the maxim that a mediator never offers professional advice can lead to an invasion of the parties' right to self-determination and a real or perceived breach of neutrality.

II. CONFIDENTIALITY:

Confidentiality is the attribute of the mediation process which promotes candor and full disclosure. Without the protection of confidentiality, parties would be unwilling to communicate freely, and the discussion necessary to resolve disputes would be seriously curtailed. Statements made during the conference and documents and other material, including a mediator's notes, generated in connection with the conference are not subject to disclosure or discovery and may not be used in a subsequent administrative or judicial proceeding. A written and executed agreement or memorandum of agreement resulting from a court-annexed or court-referred ADR process is discoverable unless the parties agree otherwise in writing. Any exceptions to the promise of confidentiality such as a statutory duty to report certain information must be revealed to the parties in the opening statement. Information given to a mediator in confidence by one party must never be revealed to another party absent permission of the first party.

Example 1: A party reveals to the mediator in caucus that he has cancer and that he does not want his ex-wife to know about it. He is not sure how long he will be working because of his illness. This information could be very important to the wife. She may need to make other plans for the time when that money is not coming in. Because of the confidentiality, the mediator feels that she cannot say anything.

Recommendation: This presents the classic dilemma of the collision between the promise of confidentiality and the need of the parties for complete information if they are to enter into an agreement voluntarily. The mediator is placed in the position of keeping a confidence of one party at the expense of the self-determination of the other party. If the mediation is terminated, there is no guarantee that the husband's condition would be revealed at trial, and the parties may lose the opportunity for a more creative agreement than the verdict imposed after a return to court.

The first tactic of the mediator is to encourage the person keeping the crucial secret to share it with the other party or allow the mediator to reveal the secret. If the secret is central to the creation of a solid agreement, and if the mediator cannot persuade the party with the crucial secret to share it, she may have no alternative but to terminate the mediation.

One mediator discussed the problem of information which, if made part of an agreement, might constitute a fraud upon the court. He felt that the ethical requirement that a lawyer is always an officer of the court would require that the lawyer/mediator not draft an agreement if there were a secret which made the agreement a fraud on the parties or on the court. "In other words, if one party says as soon as we sign this custody agreement I'm going to take my kids across the country, that would put me in an impossible conflict of interest. I would feel that I would be perpetrating a fraud on the other side if I allowed them to enter into an agreement."

Example 2: *A deceptively simple example of this problem can occur in jurisdictions where a "warrant fee" must be paid even if the warrant is not served or is dropped. As the parties enter into the mediation of this subissue after the mediation of the dispute which resulted in the warrant is completed, both parties refuse to pay a penny, saying that it is the responsibility of the other party. In caucus, one party says "I'll pay half of it but don't tell them that." Or someone will say, "I think I should only have to pay half of it, but I'd pay it all to be finished with this, but don't tell them." The mediator has been given a piece of information that would make a difference in the settlement of perhaps the entire case and instructed not to tell.*

Recommendation: When the secret information is something that would foster settlement rather than something that would prevent settlement, the mediator is remiss if he or she does not push the parties toward revelation.

An interesting problem intersecting self-determination and confidentiality occurs because of the increasing use of guardians ad litem to represent the interests of the child in disputed custody cases. If the guardian is present at the mediation, should he or she be privy to the entire mediation, including caucuses? The interests of the child are not necessarily synonymous with the positions of parties. One solution to the issue would be to caucus separately with each party and with the guardian. Another question is whether the guardian, who has an obligation to report to the court, can be bound by confidentiality.

Recommendation: The mediator's opening statement should include an explanation that the guardian ad litem is a party to the mediation whose interests may be separate from those of the other parties. Parties should be informed of the limits on confidentiality presented by the guardian ad litem's presence in the joint session. The mediator should caucus with the guardian ad litem separately. The guardian ad litem should not be present when the mediator conducts a caucus with a party.

III. IMPARTIALITY:

A mediator must demonstrate impartiality in word and deed. A mediator must scrupulously avoid any appearance of partiality.

Example 1: As one mediator expressed this problem: "I had a big case once upon a time where I thought the plaintiffs, who were represented by three attorneys, had made a very poor presentation of their case and this was a case that went on for multiple sessions. I don't remember whether it was the opening presentation. I think it may not have been the opening presentation, but a subsequent presentation, and it may have been on just a few issues or something like that. I felt like they did not present their case in as strong a form as they could have. Maybe that they were holding back some evidence. In caucus I just did some coaching. I don't mean to be so presumptuous as to say that I knew how to do it better than they did but I pointed out some things to them that I think they agreed with. They went back and made a more forceful, more cogent presentation and I think were able to move things along better. Because by making a weak presentation of their case, they were not going to be able to get what they knew or believed they were entitled to. So it was a matter of helping the other side see the strengths of the plaintiff's case that they had not been able to see through the original presentation."

Recommendation: *Several mediators discussed the problem of dealing with a party who is unable to bargain effectively and puzzled over an ethical way to coach that party while retaining neutrality. Helping a party to present his or her needs and interests in a way that can be heard by the other side is not a breach of neutrality but is, rather, an important part of the mediator's role. When the mediator helps each side to communicate effectively, the mediator is assisting the parties in establishing the common ground upon which a solid agreement can be based.*

Commentary: *Mediators gave very few examples of situations in which they felt such antipathy for a party that they were unable to remain neutral. Many mediators discussed the fact that when they began to search for needs and interests of a party they were able to reach a sufficient level of understanding that neutrality was not an issue.*

Although the classic dilemma regarding impartiality occurs when the mediator feels great sympathy or antipathy toward one party or another, the problem is more complicated when the loss of impartiality occurs because of behavior of someone other than a party.

Example 1: During a mediation the attorneys begin to fight with each other to the extent that it is difficult to control the mediation. It is also difficult for the mediator to keep an open mind about how to deal with it because, as he expressed his own emotion, his stomach is churning. The mediator is faced not only with controlling the situation but in dealing with his own reaction to it. The mediation did not result in an agreement although the matter was settled before trial. The mediator wondered in hindsight if it might have been better if he had said "Look, because of the way I'm reacting to your fight, I can't be an effective mediator for you. You need a different personality to help you mediate."

A. A mediator must reveal any connection with a party or attorney which would cause or appear to cause an occasion for bias. Mediators should avoid any dual relationship with a party which would cause any question about the mediator's impartiality.

B. A mediator may not accept anything of value from a party or attorney for a party before, during, or after the mediation, other than the compensation agreed upon. Mediators should be sensitive to the fact that future business dealings with parties may give the appearance of impropriety. However, it is not improper for a mediator to receive referrals from parties or attorneys.

Example 1: A divorce mediation results in a full agreement The parties do not want to take the agreement and spend the extra money on an attorney. And they ask the mediator to take the agreement to court and help them obtain an uncontested divorce. As the mediator described the problem, "I told them that technically I could but no I won't because I've been your mediator and must be neutral. I think it would be a conflict for me to go from mediator to attorney in the same case for the purpose of getting you your divorce and making it legal. They said that they really didn't want to go pay anybody else and asked me to prepare the papers. So I charged them an additional fee to prepare the papers, the decree and separation agreement, without my name on it and I told them to file it pro se. They were satisfied with that and I could sleep with that decision."

Recommendation: The ethical problems that arise in the area of subsequent contact with parties have to do with neutrality and the perception that the mediator might capitalize upon the mediation experience to create a future business relationship with one or the other party. Here the mediator did legal work for both parties so that there was no question of a breach of neutrality. There was no question that the dual representation was clearly explained and understood by the parties. Further, the mediator tried to distance himself by refusing to represent the parties in court, acting more as a scribe than a representative. He acted with great reluctance and only because the parties requested that they not be placed in a position of incurring additional expense. This mediator said that specific rules in this area would be helpful. It is the Commission's recommendation that a lawyer/mediator never accept any legal work arising out of the mediation. In the context of the example above, this recommendation is more for the protection of the mediator than for the parties.

IV. FAIRNESS:

The mediator is the guardian of fairness of the process. In that context, the mediator must assure that the conference is characterized by overall fairness and must protect the integrity of the process.

A. A mediator should not be a party to an agreement which is illegal or impossible to execute. The mediator should alert parties to the effect of the agreement upon third parties who are not part of the mediation. The mediator should alert the parties to the problems which may arise if the effectiveness of the agreement depends upon the commitment of persons who are not parties to the agreement. A mediator may refuse to draft or sign an agreement which seems fundamentally unfair to one party.

Commentary: Georgia mediators expressed two concerns related to the fairness of a mediated agreement: How to handle the situation in which the parties agree to something which the mediator feels is unworkable; how to separate out the mediator's own bias that a party could have done better from the agreement which seems fundamentally unfair to the party.

Example 1: *As one mediator expressed the tension, "You know, have you done this or that? Why don't we come back? 'No, I just want to get it over with.' God, you're paying such a price just to get it over with. But then, maybe they just really need to get it over with. I don't know how many times I've heard that, that I just want to get it over with. I don't care what it takes, I want it done, nobody's going to abide by this anyway. Whatever that whole bundle of things may be. That's my bugaboo. I don't know what advice to give other people about it. You can create some type of abstract standard [for mediators to handle this situation.]"*

Example 2: *In a juvenile court case the parties are working toward agreement and the mediator realizes that the child is agreeing to anything in order to get out of the room. The mediator also realizes that if the agreement is breached, the child will have to answer for the breach in court. The mediator's reality testing is to no avail.*

Example 3: *The mediator is concerned about the tax consequences of a property transfer, and the parties are unwilling to consult an outside expert. As one mediator set forth the problem: "So they come in with a house to sell or a business as part of their marital assets and you're talking about transferring all this property and then what about the taxes. Have you thought about the tax implications? They say no, and you say well you ought to go see a CPA and get this information. And they don't want to because they don't want to spend any more money and all of a sudden you're taking what appeared to be a simple situation and you're making it more complex and you're making it more expensive and where does it stop. That's our question."*

Example 4: *The parties have been married twenty-two years and have grown children. They come to mediation having settled everything but who is to get the Volvo, which is for them their most prestigious material possession. The husband suggests the solution of just selling the car, a solution which would make it possible to finalize the divorce. The wife, who is not ready for finality, begins to cry hysterically and then says "Just write it up and I'll sign anything."*

Recommendation: The mediator's tension may result from his or her concern that the agreement is not the best possible agreement. On the other end of the continuum, the mediator feels that the agreement is unconscionable. This is an area in which the mediator's sense of fairness may collide with the fundamental principle of self-determination of the parties. On the other end of a continuum, the mediator may feel that the agreement is unfair in that one party is not fully informed. In other words, the process by which agreement was reached was unfair because one party was not bargaining from a position of knowledge. An underlying question is whose yardstick should be used in measuring fairness.

The mediator has an obligation to test the parties' understanding of the agreement by making sure that they understand all that it involves and the ramifications of the agreement. The mediator has an obligation to make sure that the parties have considered the effect of the agreement upon third parties. If after testing the agreement the mediator is convinced that the agreement is so unfair that he or she cannot participate, the mediator should withdraw without drafting the agreement. Parties should be informed that they are, of course, free to enter into any agreement that they wish notwithstanding the withdrawal of the mediator.

B. A mediator is the guardian of the integrity of the mediation process.

Commentary: Georgia mediators expressed concern about confusion of parties and neutrals as to the difference between various ADR processes. This confusion may result in the parties' not knowing what to expect of the mediation process. While there is room for variation in mediation style from the more directive to the more therapeutic, the mediator should recognize the line between mediation and a more evaluative process and be prepared to refer the party to another process if that would be more appropriate.

Another concern mentioned by many Georgia mediators was how to recognize impasse and, perhaps more difficult, how to recognize when parties come to the table unwilling to bargain in good faith. Another variation on this theme is the attorney who has come to the

*table merely intending to benefit from free discovery or use media-
tion as a dilatory tactic. Yet another variation on this theme was the
expectation of lawyers that the mediation could be completed in one
session. These problems are experienced differently whether the
mediator is being compensated on an hourly basis, per session, or is a
volunteer. Many mediators and program directors struggle with the
issue of good faith and the question of whether lack of good faith can
ever by reported to the court.*

*Recommendation: When a mediator realizes that a party is not
bargaining in good faith, he or she often experiences an understandable frustration and a desire to report the bad faith to the
court. The pledge of confidentiality extends to the question of
conduct in the mediation, excepting of course threatened or
actual violence. The possible damage to the process by reporting
more than offsets the benefit in a given case. Further, if the lode-
star of mediation is the principle of self-determination, the
unwillingness of a party to bargain in good faith is consistent
with that party's right to refuse the benefits of mediation.*

V. RULES OF FAIR PRACTICE:

Referrals

Mediators should observe the same care to be impartial in their
business dealings that they observe in the mediation session. In
this regard, mediators should not refer parties to any entity in
which they have any economic interest. As a corollary to this
principle, mediators should avoid referrals to professionals from
whom the mediator expects to receive future business. Similarly,
mediators should avoid an ongoing referral relationship with an
attorney that would interfere with that attorney's independent
judgment.

It is not improper to receive referrals from attorneys or parties.
However, mediators should be aware that their impartiality or
appearance of impartiality may be compromised by referrals
from parties or attorneys for whom they act as mediators on
more than one occasion.

Fees

Mediators who are compensated by parties must be scrupulous in disclosing all fees and costs at the earliest opportunity. Fees may be based on an hourly rate, a sliding scale, or a set fee for an entire mediation as long as the fee structure has been carefully explained to the parties and they have consented to the arrangement.

Fees may never be contingent upon a specific result. It is imperative that the mediator have no "stake" in the outcome.

Mediators who serve for compensation in court programs are obligated to provide some pro bono hours in order to serve parties who are indigent.

Competence

Mediators are obligated to disclose their training and background to parties who request such information. Mediators are obligated not to undertake cases for which their training or expertise is inadequate.

Mediators who serve in court programs or receive referrals from courts must be registered with the Georgia Office of Dispute Resolution and must be in compliance with the Alternative Dispute Resolution Rules of the Supreme Court of Georgia. Any mediator who receives a court referral without being in compliance with the Supreme Court Rules is subject to being removed from the registry of the Georgia Office of Dispute Resolution. Further, the immunity protection of the Supreme Court Rules is not available to mediators who receive court referrals without being in compliance with said rules.

Advertising

Mediators are permitted to advertise. Mediators have an obligation to the integrity of the mediation process. In that regard, all statements as to qualifications must be truthful. Mediators may never claim that they will guarantee a specific result. It is important to the public perception of mediation that advertisements by mediators are not only accurate, clear, and truthful, but that they are in no way misleading.

Diligence

Mediators will exercise diligence in scheduling the mediation, drafting the agreement if requested to do so, and returning completed necessary paperwork to the court or referring agency.

Mediation may be terminated by either the mediator or the parties at any time. Mediators will be sensitive to the need to terminate the mediation if an impasse has been reached. However, mediators must be courageous in declaring impasse only when there is no possibility of progress.

APPENDIX E

THE CODE OF ETHICS FOR ARBITRATORS IN COMMERCIAL DISPUTES[93]

(Revised 1999)

The original Code of Ethics for Arbitrators in Commercial Disputes was prepared in 1977 by a joint committee consisting of a special committee of the American Arbitration Association and a special committee of the American Bar Association.

This 1999 Revision of the Code was prepared by a Committee convened by the Arbitration Committee of the Section of Dispute Resolution of the American Bar Association and including representatives of the American Arbitration Association and CPR Institute for Dispute Resolution.

The Drafting Committee seeks approval and recommendation by the participating organizations and other organizations that provide, coordinate or administer the services of arbitrators. By doing so such organizations will provide ethical guidance for their arbitration panel members. The Drafting Committee deems it important that ethical standards be developed for such organizations as well but did not take any action on this subject pending the development of standards undertaken by the Working Group for ADR Provider Organizations convened by the CPR-Georgetown Commission on Ethics and Standards in ADR.

The views expressed herein have not yet been approved by the ABA House of Delegates or the Board of Governors of the American Bar Association and accordingly should not be construed as representing the policy of the American Bar Association.

---

93. ©2002. Reprinted with permission of the American Arbitration Association and the American Bar Association.

The Code of Ethics for Arbitrators in Commercial Disputes

(1998 Revision)

PREAMBLE

The use of commercial arbitration to resolve a wide variety of disputes forms a significant part of the system of justice on which our society relies for fair determination of legal rights. Persons who act as commercial arbitrators therefore undertake serious responsibilities to the public as well as to the parties. Those responsibilities include important ethical obligations.

Few cases of unethical behavior by commercial arbitrators have arisen. Nevertheless, the American Bar Association and the American Arbitration Association believe that it is in the public interest to set forth generally accepted standards of ethical conduct for guidance of arbitrators and parties in commercial disputes. By establishing this Code, the sponsors hope to contribute to the maintenance of high standards and continued confidence in the process of arbitration.

There are many different types of commercial arbitration. Some cases are conducted under arbitration rules established by various organizations and trade associations, while others are conducted without such rules. The Federal Arbitration Act (9 U.S.C. §§ 1, et seq.), the Uniform Arbitration Act and other bodies of state or local law control some critically important aspects of the arbitration process and provide default procedures and guidance as to other aspects. Although most cases are arbitrated pursuant to voluntary agreement of the parties, certain types of disputes are submitted to arbitration by reason of particular laws. This Code is intended to apply to all such proceedings in which disputes or claims are submitted for decision to one or more arbitrators appointed in a manner provided by agreement of the parties, by applicable arbitration rules, or by law. In all such cases, the persons who have the power to decide should observe fundamental standards of ethical conduct. In this Code all such persons are called "arbitrators" although, in some types of cases, they might be called "umpires," "referees," "neutrals," or have some other title.

Various aspects of the conduct of arbitrators, including some matters covered by this Code, may be governed by agreements of the parties, by arbitration rules to which the parties have agreed, or by applicable law. This Code does not take the place of or supersede such agreements, rules, or laws and does not establish new or additional grounds for judicial review of arbitration awards. It is intended to provide standards of conduct for arbitrators that will maintain the apparent integrity, perceived fairness and other necessary or desirable characteristics of the arbitration process. It should be so perceived by individual arbitrators when acting as such, and also by organizations that provide, coordinate or administer the services of arbitrators.

This Code is intended to provide ethical guidelines to all individuals serving as commercial arbitrators. In those instances where it has been approved and recommended by organizations that provide, coordinate or administer services of arbitrators it is intended to provide ethical standards for the members of their respective panels of commercial arbitrators. However it does not form a part of the arbitration rules of any such organization. Nor is it intended to apply to persons engaged in such processes as mediation, conciliation, court-annexed arbitration, mini-trial or early neutral evaluation. Labor arbitration is governed by the Code of Professional Responsibility for Arbitrators of Labor-Management Disputes, not by this Code. While institutions that provide, coordinate or administer the services of arbitrators are not governed by this Code, it is expected that they will take into account the guidelines in this Code in the performance of their administrative functions.

Arbitrators, like judges, have the power to decide cases. However, unlike full-time judges, arbitrators are usually engaged in other occupations before, during, and after the time that they serve as arbitrators. Often, arbitrators are purposely chosen from the same trade or industry as the parties in order to bring special knowledge to the task of deciding. This Code recognizes these fundamental differences between arbitrators and judges.

In some types of arbitration there are three or more arbitrators. The Code on occasion refers to multiple-arbitrator panels as "the arbitrator." In some cases, it is the practice for each party, acting alone, to appoint one arbitrator and for the other arbitrator to be designated by those two, by the parties, or by an independent institution or individual. The sponsors of this Code believe that it is preferable for parties to agree that all arbitrators should comply with the same ethical standards. However, it is recognized that there is a long-established practice in some types of arbitration for the arbitrators who are appointed by one party, acting alone, to be governed by special ethical considerations. Those special considerations are set forth in the last section of the Code, headed "Ethical Considerations Relating to Arbitrators Appointed by One Party."

The Code refers to the parties to arbitration and to their representatives collectively as "parties."

Although this Code is expected to be sponsored by the American Bar Association and the American Arbitration Association and other institutions, its use is not limited to arbitrations administered by such institutions or to cases in which the arbitrators are lawyers. Rather, it is presented as a public service to provide guidance in all types of commercial arbitration.

I. THE ARBITRATOR SHOULD UPHOLD THE INTEGRITY AND FAIRNESS OF THE ARBITRATION PROCESS.

A. Fair and just processes for resolving disputes are indispensable in our society. Commercial arbitration is an important method for deciding many types of disputes. In order for commercial arbitration to be effective, there must be broad public confidence in the integrity and fairness of the process. Therefore, an arbitrator has a responsibility not only to the parties but also to the process of arbitration itself, and must observe high standards of conduct so that the integrity and fairness of the process will be preserved. Accordingly, the arbitrator should recognize a responsibility to the public, to the parties whose rights will be decided, and to all other participants in the proceeding.

The provisions of this Code should be construed and applied to further these objectives.

B. One should accept appointment as an arbitrator only if fully satisfied (1) of his or her ability to serve without bias; (2) that he or she is competent to serve; and (3) that he or she can be available to commence the arbitration in accordance with the requirements of the case and thereafter to give to it the time and attention to its completion that the parties are reasonably entitled to expect.

C. After accepting appointment and while serving as arbitrator a person should avoid entering into any financial, business, professional, family or social relationship, or acquiring any financial or personal interest, which is likely to affect impartiality or which might reasonably create the appearance of partiality or bias. For a reasonable period of time after the decision of a case, persons who have served as arbitrators should avoid entering into any such relationship, or acquiring any such interest, in circumstances which might reasonably create the appearance that they had been influenced in the arbitration by the anticipation or expectation of the relationship or interest.

D. Arbitrators should conduct themselves in a way that is fair to all parties and should not be swayed by outside pressure, by public clamor, by fear of criticism or by self-interest. They should avoid conduct and statements that give the appearance of partiality toward any party. They should guard against partiality or prejudice based on any party's personal characteristics, background or performance at the arbitration.

E. When an arbitrator's authority is derived from an agreement of the parties, the arbitrator should neither exceed that authority nor do less than is required to exercise that authority completely. Where the agreement of the parties sets forth procedures to be followed in conducting the arbitration or refers to rules to be followed, it is the obligation of the arbitrator to comply with such procedures or rules. The arbitrator has no obligation to comply with any such procedures or rules that are unlawful, unconscionable, or inconsistent with this Code.

F. The arbitrator should make all reasonable efforts to assure the prompt, economical and fair resolution of the matters submitted for decision. The arbitrator should endeavor to prevent delaying tactics, harassment of parties or other participants, or other abuse or disruption of the arbitration process.

G. The ethical obligations of an arbitrator begin upon acceptance of the appointment and continue throughout all stages of the proceeding. In addition, wherever specifically set forth in this Code, certain ethical obligations begin as soon as a person is requested to serve as an arbitrator and certain ethical obligations continue even after the decision in the case has been given to the parties.

Comment to Canon I

One is not impartial and should not serve as a neutral arbitrator when he or she favors one of the parties or is prejudiced in relation to the subject matter of the dispute. A potential arbitrator does not become partial or prejudiced by having acquired knowledge of the parties or of the applicable law or of the customs and practices of the business involved. A potential arbitrator is partial or prejudiced if, for example, prior to appointment he or she for any reason has formed an opinion as to the appropriate outcome of the case.

Existence of any of the matters or circumstances described in subparagraphs C or D of Canon I does not render it unethical for one to serve as a neutral arbitrator where the parties have consented to the arbitrator's appointment or continued service following full disclosure of the relevant facts in accordance with Canon II. The matters set forth in subparagraph B of Canon I reflect the arbitrator's obligation to the public and to the process, and therefore reflect circumstances where it is inappropriate for a neutral arbitrator to serve as such even though the parties have voiced no objection to the appointment or continued service following full disclosure.

During an arbitration, the arbitrator may be expected to engage in discourse with the parties or their counsel, to draw out arguments or contentions, to comment on the law or the evidence, to make interim rulings, and otherwise to control or direct the arbitration. These activities are integral parts of an active adjudicative process. Subparagraph D of Canon I is not intended to preclude or limit either full discussion of the issues during the course of the arbitration or the arbitrator's management of the proceeding.

If an arbitrator is a member of a law firm or a business organization, the arbitrator should endeavor to assure that the firm or organization does not enter into or structure relationships which may affect the arbitrator's neutrality or create a reasonable appearance of partiality, bias or post-award remuneration.

II. AN ARBITRATOR SHOULD DISCLOSE ANY INTEREST OR RELATIONSHIP LIKELY TO AFFECT IMPARTIALITY OR WHICH MIGHT CREATE AN APPEARANCE OF PARTIALITY OR BIAS.

A. Persons who are requested to serve as arbitrators should, before accepting, disclose

(1) any direct or indirect financial or personal interest in the outcome of the arbitration which is known or becomes known;

(2) any existing or past financial, business, professional, family or social relationships which are known or become known and are likely to affect impartiality or which might reasonably create an appearance of partiality of bias. Prospective arbitrators should disclose any such relationships which they personally have with any party or its lawyer, with any party-appointed arbitrator, or with any individual whom they have been told will be a witness. They should also disclose any such relationships involving their immediate family or household members or their current employers, partners or professional or business associates;

(3) the nature and extent of any prior knowledge he or she may have of the dispute; and

(4) any other matters, relationships or interests which they are obligated to disclose by the agreement of the parties, the rules or

practices of the institution which is administering the arbitration, or applicable law regulating arbitrator disclosure.

B. Persons who are requested to accept appointments as arbitrators should make a reasonable effort to inform themselves of any interests or relationships described in the preceding subparagraph A.

C. The obligation to disclose interests or relationships described in the preceding subparagraphs A and B is a continuing duty which requires a person who accepts appointment as an arbitrator to disclose forthwith, at any stage of the arbitration, any such interests or relationships which may arise, or which are recalled or discovered.

D. Disclosure should be made to all parties unless other procedures for disclosure are provided in the agreement of the parties, the rules or practices of the institution which is administering the arbitration, or by law. Where more than one arbitrator has been appointed, each should inform the others of the interests and relationships which have been disclosed.

E. In the event that an arbitrator is requested by all parties to withdraw, the arbitrator should do so. In the event that an arbitrator is requested to withdraw by less than all of the parties because of alleged partiality or bias, the arbitrator should withdraw unless either of the following circumstances exists:

(1) If an agreement of the parties, arbitration rules agreed to by the parties, or applicable law establishes procedures for determining challenges to arbitrators, then those procedures should be followed; or,

(2) If the arbitrator, after carefully considering the matter, determines that the reason for the challenge is not substantial, and that he or she can nevertheless act and decide the case impartially and fairly, and that withdrawal would cause unfair delay or expense to another party or would be contrary to the ends of justice.

F. Nothing contained in this Code shall require or be deemed to require any arbitrator or prospective arbitrator to disclose any confidential or privileged information without the consent of the person who furnished the information or the holder of the privilege.

Comment to Canon II

This Canon reflects the prevailing principle that arbitrators should disclose the existence of interests or relationships that are likely to affect their impartiality or that might reasonably create an appearance that they are biased against one party or favorable to another. These provisions of this Canon are intended to be applied realistically so that the burden of detailed disclosure does not become so great that it is impractical for persons in the business or legal worlds to be arbitrators, thereby depriving parties of the services of those who might be best informed and qualified to decide particular types of cases.

Except as provided in the Comment to Canon I, Canon II does not limit the freedom of parties to agree on whomever they choose as an arbitrator. When parties, with knowledge of a person's interests and relationships, nevertheless desire that individual to serve as an arbitrator, that person may properly serve.

Comment to Subparagraph A.

Although Canon II identifies interests and relationships which should be the subject of disclosure, there may also be matters in a proposed arbitrator's background or experience which so closely parallel facts asserted or proved in the arbitration that if known by the parties might give rise to a reasonable appearance of bias, and thus should be disclosed.

Comment to Subparagraph B.

The scope of a reasonable effort to become informed depends upon the circumstances. A single standard cannot be established for all situations. As a general proposition an inquiry by a member of a firm or business organization should encompass the current or recent business or professional relationships of his or her employers, partners and associates as well.

Comment to Subparagraph E.

Since arbitration generally exists by virtue of agreement between or among the parties to submit their disputes to a non-judicial forum, it is appropriate that an arbitrator withdraw upon the request of all parties. If the arbitrator has disclosed to the parties in advance that a fee will be charged if time has been set aside for the arbitration and cannot be filled, in accordance with Canon VII, a cancellation or termination charge is not improper.

In applying the provisions of Paragraph E in the circumstance where less than all of the parties have requested that the arbitrator withdraw, the institution that is administering the arbitration and is charged with responsibility for passing upon the request, if one exists, or the arbitrator in a non-administered proceeding, should consider the timeliness of the request. Where the arbitrator has had minimal involvement in the case it may be preferable that the arbitrator withdraw. If the matter has proceeded to the point where substantial time and effort have been devoted to hearings and withdrawal will result in duplication of effort, significant expense, and significant delay in resolving the matter, the prejudice to the non-objecting party must be weighed against the credibility and seriousness of the basis for the request.

Although the Canons are for the guidance of arbitrators, not parties, the role of the parties should be noted. If a party is aware of material interests or relationships that the arbitrator has not disclosed or has overlooked, it is preferable that these be made known to the other parties or arbitrators or to the tribunal if one exists. In considering an untimely request for withdrawal the arbitrator or tribunal may properly consider whether the requesting party was aware of the claimed relationship or interest at the time the arbitrator was appointed or delayed unduly in presenting its request after acquiring such knowledge, to the prejudice of non-objecting parties.

III. AN ARBITRATOR IN COMMUNICATING WITH THE PARTIES SHOULD AVOID IMPROPRIETY OR THE APPEARANCE OF IMPROPRIETY.

A. If an agreement of the parties or applicable arbitration rules establishes the manner or content of communications between the arbitrator and the parties, the arbitrator should follow those procedures notwithstanding any contrary provision of the following subparagraphs B and C.

B. Unless otherwise provided in applicable arbitration rules or in an agreement of the parties, arbitrators should not discuss a case with any party in the absence of any other party, except in any of the following circumstances:

(1) When the appointment of a prospective arbitrator is being considered, the prospective arbitrator (a) may ask about the identity of parties or witnesses and the general nature of the case; and (b) may respond to inquiries from the parties or their counsel designed to determine his or her suitability and availability for the appointment. In any such dialogue the prospective arbitrator may receive information disclosing the general nature of the dispute, but should not permit the parties or their representatives the opportunity to argue the merits of the case.

(2) In an arbitration in which the two party-appointed arbitrators are expected to appoint the third arbitrator, each party-appointed arbitrator may consult with the party who appointed the arbitrator concerning the acceptability of persons under consideration for appointment as the third arbitrator.

(3) Discussions may be had with a party concerning such matters as setting the time and place of hearings or making other arrangements for the conduct of the proceedings. However, the arbitrator should promptly inform any other party of the discussion and should not make any final determination concerning the matter discussed before giving any absent party an opportunity to express the party's views.

(4) If a party fails to be present at a hearing after having been given due notice, the arbitrator may discuss the case with any party who is present.

(5) If all parties request or consent to it, such discussion may take place.

C. Unless otherwise provided in applicable arbitration rules or in an agreement of the parties, whenever an arbitrator communicates in writing with one party, the arbitrator should at the same time send a copy of the communication to every other party, and, whenever the arbitrator receives any written communication concerning the case from one party which has not already been sent to every other party, the arbitrator should send or cause it to be sent to the other parties.

IV. AN ARBITRATOR SHOULD CONDUCT THE PROCEEDINGS FAIRLY AND DILIGENTLY.

A. The arbitrator should conduct the proceedings in an even-handed manner and treat all parties with equality and fairness at all stages of the proceedings.

B. The arbitrator should perform duties diligently and conclude the case as promptly as the circumstances reasonably permit.

C. The arbitrator should be patient and courteous to the parties, to their representatives and to the witnesses and should encourage similar conduct by all participants in the proceedings.

D. Unless otherwise agreed by the parties or provided in applicable arbitration rules, the arbitrator should afford to all parties the right to appear in person and to be heard after due notice of the time and place of any hearing or pre-hearing conference. At any evidentiary hearing, the arbitrator should allow each party fair opportunity to present its evidence and arguments. The arbitrator may preclude evidence which is irrelevant or cumulative.

E. The arbitrator should not deny any party the opportunity to be represented by counsel.

F. If a party fails to appear after due notice, the arbitrator should proceed with the arbitration when authorized to do so by the agreement of the parties, the applicable rules or by law. However, the arbitrator should do so only after receiving assurance that appropriate notice has been given to the absent party.

G. When the arbitrator determines that more information than has been presented by the parties is required to decide the case, it is not improper for the arbitrator to ask questions, call witnesses, and request documents or other evidence.

H. It is not improper for an arbitrator to suggest to the parties that they discuss the possibility of settlement of the case or the use of mediation, conciliation or other dispute resolution processes. However, an arbitrator should not be present or otherwise participate in the settlement discussions or such other processes unless requested to do so by all parties. An arbitrator should not exert pressure on any party to settle or to utilize other dispute resolution processes.

I. Nothing in this Code is intended to prevent a person from acting as a mediator or conciliator of a dispute in which he or she has been appointed as arbitrator, if requested to do so by all parties or where authorized or required to do so by applicable laws or rules.

J. When there is more than one arbitrator, the arbitrators should afford each other the full opportunity to participate in all aspects of the proceedings.

Comment to Canon IV

Subparagraph J of Canon IV is not intended to preclude one arbitrator from acting in limited circumstances (i.e., ruling on discovery issues) where authorized by the agreement of the parties or applicable rules or law. Nor does it preclude a majority of the arbitrators from proceeding with any aspect of the arbitration if an arbitrator is unable or unwilling to participate and such action is authorized by the agreement of the parties or applicable rules or law.

V. AN ARBITRATOR SHOULD MAKE DECISIONS IN A JUST, INDEPENDENT AND DELIBERATE MANNER.

A. The arbitrator should, after careful deliberation, decide all issues submitted for determination. The arbitrator should decide no other issues.

B. The arbitrator should decide all matters justly, exercising independent judgment, and should not permit outside pressure to affect the decision.

C. The arbitrator should not delegate the duty to decide to any other person.

D. In the event that all parties agree upon a settlement of issues in dispute and request the arbitrator to embody that agreement in an award, the arbitrator may do so, but is not required to do so unless satisfied with the propriety of the terms of settlement. Whenever the arbitrator embodies a settlement by the parties in an award, the arbitrator should state in the award that it is based on an agreement of the parties.

Comment to Canon V, Subparagraph C

Subparagraph C does not preclude an arbitrator from obtaining help from an associate or from a research, clerical or other assistant in connection with reaching his or her decision, so long as such assistants agree to be bound by the provisions of subparagraphs A, B and C of Canon VI.

VI. AN ARBITRATOR SHOULD BE FAITHFUL TO THE RELATIONSHIP OF TRUST AND CONFIDENTIALITY INHERENT IN THAT OFFICE.

A. An arbitrator is in a relationship of trust to the parties and should not, at any time, use or disclose confidential information acquired during the arbitration proceedings to gain personal advantage or advantage for others, or to affect adversely the interest of another.

B. Unless otherwise agreed by the parties or required by applicable rules or law, the arbitrator should keep confidential all matters relating to the arbitration proceedings and decision.

C. It is not proper at any time for an arbitrator to inform anyone of the decision in advance of the time it is given to all parties, with the exception of an organization which is administering the arbitration, under applicable rules or procedures. In a case in which there is more than one arbitrator, it is not proper at any time for an arbitrator to inform anyone concerning the deliberations of the arbitrators. After an arbitration award has been made, it is not proper for an arbitrator to assist in postarbitral proceedings, except as is required by applicable rules or law or by the terms of the award, or if the parties agree that the arbitrator may do so.

D. Except where otherwise agreed by the parties or required by applicable rules or law, when the award has been made the arbitrator may offer to return all evidentiary materials to the producing parties or their representatives. If the offer is not accepted, following due notice, the arbitrator may dispose of such materials in any manner reasonably calculated to prevent their use or disclosure.

Comment to Canon VI

Unless the parties so request, an arbitrator should not appoint himself or herself to a separate office related to the subject matter of the dispute, such as receiver or trustee, nor should a panel of arbitrators appoint one of their number to such office.

VII. AN ARBITRATOR'S ARRANGEMENTS FOR COMPENSATION AND REIMBURSEMENT OF EXPENSES SHOULD BE FAIR AND CLEARLY DISCLOSED TO ALL PARTIES.

In some types of arbitration it is customary practice for the arbitrators to serve without pay. In other cases, however, arbitrators receive compensation for their services and reimbursement for their expenses. In making arrangements for such payments all persons who are requested to serve or who are serving as arbitrators should be governed by the same high standards of integrity and fairness as apply to their other activities in the case. Accordingly, such persons should avoid any communications concerning the amount of or matters pertaining to such payments which would create an appearance of coercion or other impropriety. In the absence of governing provisions in the agreement of the parties or in applicable rules or law, certain practices relating to payments are generally recognized as being preferable in order to preserve the integrity and fairness of the arbitration process. These practices include the following.

(1) It is preferable that, before the arbitrator finally accepts appointment, the terms and conditions of payment, including cancellation fees and compensation for study and preparation time, be established and that all parties be informed thereof in writing.

(2) In cases conducted under the rules or administration of an institution that is available to assist in making arrangements for payments, the payments should be arranged by the institution to avoid the necessity for communication by the arbitrators directly with the parties concerning the subject.

(3) In cases where no institution has been engaged by the parties to administer the arbitration, it is preferable that any communication with arbitrators concerning payments take place in writing or in the presence of all parties.

(4) Absent extraordinary circumstances, the arbitrator should not ask that his or her rate of compensation be increased during the pendency of the arbitration.

VIII. AN ARBITRATOR MAY ENGAGE IN ADVERTISING OR PROMOTION OF ARBITRAL SERVICES IN A DISCREET AND PROFESSIONAL MANNER.

Advertising or promotion of an arbitrator's willingness or availability to serve as such should be limited to the statement that he or she is an arbitrator, a brief description of his or her professional credentials, experience, and relevant areas of expertise or activities, and such information as may be required to facilitate contact and communication. Such advertising or promotion must not (a) be inaccurate or likely to mislead; (b) make comparison with other arbitrators or members of other professions; (c) include statements about the quality of the arbitrator's work or the success of the arbitrator's practice; or (d) imply any willingness to accept an appointment otherwise than in accordance with this Code. This Canon does not preclude an arbitrator, from printing, publishing or disseminating advertisements conforming to the foregoing standards in any electronic or print medium, from making personal presentations to prospective users of arbitral services conforming to such standards, or from responding to inquiries concerning the arbitrator's availability, qualifications, experience or fee arrangements.

IX. THE AWARD SHOULD BE CLEAR, COMPLETE AND EFFECTIVE.

The arbitrator's award should conform to any requirements of the agreement of the parties. To the extent practicable it should be drafted in plain English, in a logical format, and in accordance with any formal requirements of applicable rules or law. All matters submitted to the arbitrator for decision should be dealt with, and each decision should be clear and explicit in order that the outcome may be legally enforceable. Except as specifically requested by the parties or provided in the agreement or applicable rules or law, the arbitrator may but need not provide the reasons leading to the arbitrator's decision.

Comment to Canon IX

The second sentence of Canon IX creates an ethical obligation to provide an award which conforms in format and structure to legal requirements (i.e. in writing, under oath if required, e.g., Uniform Arbitration Act, § 8). The Code takes no position as to whether an arbitrator has any ethical obligation to render an award that conforms to applicable principles of substantive law.

An arbitrator should prepare a written statement of reasons for his or her award or a reasoned award if (1) the arbitration agreement or applicable rules or law require the arbitrator to do so; or (2) all parties request or stipulate that the arbitrator do so.

In all other circumstances the arbitrator should take the following factors into account in determining whether or not to prepare a written statement of reasons or a reasoned award: (1) the nature and importance of the legal or economic issues presented by the case; (2) any need for such statement or award as a guide to the parties in conducting their future affairs; (3) any need for such statement or award as a guide to the parties in dealing with the rights or obligations of third parties; (4) whether or to what extent the award may serve as a legal or business precedent; and (5) the additional cost to the parties, if any, for the arbitrator's services in preparing such statement or award, weighed against any additional benefit to be derived from it.

X. ETHICAL CONSIDERATIONS RELATING TO ARBITRATORS APPOINTED BY ONE PARTY.

A. Disclosure of Status

In all arbitrations in which there are two or more party-appointed arbitrators, each party-appointed arbitrator should inform the other arbitrators forthwith following appointment that he or she is party-appointed, whether he or she is to be neutral, and whether he or she will or will not observe those obligations which are excused by subparagraphs A, B, C and E of this Canon X, unless (i) all parties have informed the arbitrators that all of the arbitrators are to be neutral or (ii) the applicable rules or law require that all arbitrators be neutral. A party-appointed arbitrator who has informed the other arbitrators that he or she is to be neutral or that he or she will observe those obligations referred to shall thereafter observe such obligations. A party-appointed arbitrator who has informed the other arbitrators that he or she will not be neutral or that he or she will not observe those obligations is referred to in this Canon X as a "non-neutral arbitrator."

B. Obligations under Canon I

Non-neutral arbitrators should observe all of the obligations of Canon I to uphold the integrity and fairness of the arbitration process, subject only to the following provisions.

(1) Non-neutral arbitrators may be predisposed toward the party who appointed them but in all other respects are obligated to act in good faith and with integrity and fairness. For example, non-neutral arbitrators should not engage in delaying tactics or harassment of any party or witness and should not knowingly make untrue or misleading statements to the other arbitrators.

(2) The provisions of subparagraphs B(1), C and D of Canon I relating to bias, relationships and interests, are not applicable to non-neutral arbitrators.

C. Obligations under Canon II

Non-neutral arbitrators should disclose to all parties and to the other arbitrators all interests and relationships which Canon II requires be disclosed. Disclosure as required by Canon II is for the benefit not only of the party who appointed the non-neutral arbitrator, but also for the benefit of the other parties and arbitrators so that they may know of any bias which may exist or appear to exist. However, non-neutral arbitrators are not obliged to withdraw if requested to do so by the party who did not appoint them, notwithstanding the provisions of subparagraph E of Canon II.

D. Obligations under Canon III

Non-neutral arbitrators should observe all of the obligations of Canon III concerning communications with the parties, subject only to the following provisions.

(1) In an arbitration in which two party-appointed arbitrators are expected to appoint the third arbitrator, party-appointed arbitrators, whether or not they are neutral, may consult with the parties who appointed them as provided in subparagraph B(2) of Canon III.

(2) Non-neutral arbitrators may communicate with the party who appointed them concerning any other aspect of the case except for matters being deliberated by the arbitrators, provided they first inform the other arbitrators and the parties that they intend to do so. If such communication occurred prior to the time the person was appointed as arbitrator, or prior to the first hearing or other meeting of the parties with the arbitrators, the non-neutral arbitrator should, at or before the first hearing or meeting, disclose the fact that such communication has taken place. In complying with the provisions of this paragraph, it is sufficient that there be disclosure of the fact that such communication has occurred without disclosing the content of the communication. A single timely disclosure of the non-neutral arbitrator's intention to participate in such communications in the future is sufficient, and there is no requirement thereafter that there be disclosure before or after each separate occasion on which such a communication occurs.

(3) When non-neutral arbitrators communicate in writing with the party who appointed them concerning any matter as to which communication is permitted under this Code, they are not required to send copies of any such written communication to any other party or arbitrator.

E. Obligations under Canon IV

Non-neutral arbitrators should observe all of the obligations of Canon IV to conduct the proceedings fairly and diligently.

F. Obligations under Canon V

Non-neutral arbitrators should observe all of the obligations of Canon V concerning making decisions, subject only to the following provision.

(1) Non-neutral arbitrators are permitted to be predisposed toward deciding in favor of the party who appointed them.

G. Obligations under Canon VI

Non-neutral arbitrators should observe all of the obligations of Canon VI to be faithful to the relationship of trust inherent in the office of arbitrator.

H. Obligations under Canon VII

Non-neutral arbitrators are not subject to the provisions of Canon VII with respect to any arrangements for payments with or payments by the party that appointed them.

I. Obligations under Canon VIII

Non-neutral arbitrators should observe all the obligations of Canon VIII concerning advertising and promotion of arbitral services.

J. Obligations under Canon IX

Non-neutral arbitrators should observe all the obligations of Canon IX concerning the form of the award.

Comment to Canon X

In some types of arbitration in which there are three arbitrators it is customary for each party, acting alone, to appoint one arbitrator. The third arbitrator is then appointed by agreement either of the parties or of the two arbitrators, or, failing such agreement, by an independent institution or individual. In some of these types of arbitration, all three arbitrators are customarily considered to be neutral and are expected to observe the same standards of ethical conduct. However, there are also many types of tripartite arbitration in which it has been the practice that the two arbitrators appointed by the parties are not considered to be neutral and are expected to observe many—but not all—of the same ethical standards as the neutral third arbitrator. For the purposes of this Code, an arbitrator appointed by one party who is not expected to observe all of the same standards as the third arbitrator is called a "non-neutral arbitrator." This Canon X describes the ethical obligations that non-neutral arbitrators should observe and those that are not applicable to them. A non-neutral arbitrator is expected to observe all of the ethical obligations prescribed by the Code with the exceptions set forth in Canon X. Non-neutral arbitrators are thus expected to adhere to the standards applicable to neutral arbitrators except as specifically excused. They too bear responsibility for the integrity and fairness of the process.

It should be noted that, in some cases, the applicable rules or laws might require that all arbitrators be neutral. In such cases, the governing rules or laws should be considered before applying any of the foregoing provisions relating to non-neutral arbitrators.

In international commercial arbitration party-appointed arbitrators are ordinarily expected to be neutral. Thus, party-appointed arbitrators in international commercial arbitration should, to the extent practicable in the circumstances, observe all of the obligations of Canons I through IX without exception.

In applying the provisions of this Code relating to disclosure, it might be helpful to recall the words of the concurring opinion, in a case decided by the US Supreme Court, that arbitrators "should err on the side of disclosure" because "it is better that the relationship be disclosed at the outset when the parties are free to reject the arbitrator or accept him with knowledge of the relationship." At the same time, it must be recognized that "an arbitrator's business relationships may be diverse indeed, involving more or less remote commercial connections with great numbers of people." Accordingly, an arbitrator "cannot be expected to provide the parties with his complete and unexpurgated business biography," nor is an arbitrator called on to disclose interests or relationships that are merely "trivial" (a concurring opinion in *Commonwealth Coatings Corp. v. Continental Casualty Co.*, 393 US 145, 151–152 (1968)).

APPENDIX F

RESOLUTION RESOURCES CORPORATION
CONTRACT FOR ARBITRATION

We, the undersigned parties (or counsel, therefore) hereby agree to submit to arbitration the following controversy:

We agree that the arbitration shall be governed by the Arbitration Rules of the Center for Public Resources as revised by Resolution Resources Corporation (RRC) which are annexed hereto.

We further agree that the above controversy shall be submitted to:

[ ] (a sole arbitrator)

[ ] (three arbitrators, of whom each party shall appoint one), or

[ ] (three arbitrators, none of whom shall be appointed by either party).

We further agree that we shall faithfully observe this agreement and the Rules and that we shall abide by and perform any award rendered by the arbitrator(s). The arbitration shall be governed by the United States Arbitration Act, 9 U.S.C. Sections 1–16, and judgment upon the award may be entered by any court having jurisdiction thereof.

The parties agree to share all fees incident to this arbitration. The arbitrator's fees incident to this arbitration shall be $ per hour per party payable to Resolution Resources Corporation at the conclusion of each daily session. An initial administrative fee of $100.00 per party is payable prior to the execution of this agreement. The decision of the arbitrator(s) will not be published until all fees are paid. The attorneys whose signatures appear below are primarily responsible for the payment of the fees in this proceeding.

Neither RRC nor any arbitrator shall be liable to any party for any act or omission in connection with any arbitration conducted under this contract or these Rules.

_____   _____

_____   _____

_____   _____

Arbitrator for RRC:

_____   _____

                                      Date

SAMPLE ONLY * * * SAMPLE ONLY * * *
SAMPLE ONLY * * *

CPR Model Agreement for Parties and Arbitrators[94]

© 2002 **CPR Institute for Dispute Resolution**, 366 Madison Avenue, New York, NY 10017-3122; (212) 949-6490, www.cpradr.org. This **excerpt** from **CPR Model Agreement for Parties and Arbitrators** reprinted with permission of **CPR Institute.**

The **CPR Institute** is a nonprofit initiative of 500 general counsel of major corporations, leading law firms and prominent legal academics whose mission is to install alternative dispute resolution (ADR) into the mainstream of legal practice.

Agreement made _____, _____
                                      (date)

between _____

represented by _____

and _____

represented by _____

and _____
                        (the Arbitrator)

A dispute has arisen between the parties (the "Dispute"). The parties have agreed to participate in an arbitration proceeding (the "Proceeding") under the CPR Rules for Non-Administered Arbitration (Revised and Effective September 15, 2000), as modified by mutual agreement (the "Procedure"), The parties have chosen the Arbitrator for the Proceeding. The parties and the Arbitrator agree as follows:

---

94. The form assumes that the arbitrator is affiliated with a law firm. If that is not the case, delete D.2. and references to the arbitrator's firm in paras. B.1 and C.

A. Duties and Obligations

1. The Arbitrator and each of the parties agree to be bound by and to comply faithfully with the Procedure.

2. The Arbitrator has no previous commitments that may significantly delay the expeditious conduct of the Proceeding and will not make any such commitments.

B. Disclosure of Prior and Existing Relationships

1. The Arbitrator has made a reasonable effort to learn and has disclosed to the parties in writing (a) all business or professional relationships the Arbitrator and/or the Arbitrator's firm have had with the parties or their law firms within the past five years, including all instances in which the Arbitrator or the Arbitrator's firm served as an attorney for any party or adverse to any party or in which the Arbitrator served as an arbitrator or mediator in a matter involving any party; (b) any financial interest the Arbitrator has in any party; (c) any significant social, business or professional relationship the Arbitrator has had with an officer or employee of a party or with an individual representing a party in the Proceeding; and (d) any other circumstances that may give rise to justifiable doubt regarding the Arbitrator's independence of impartiality in the Proceeding.

2. Each party and its law firm has made a reasonable effort to learn and has disclosed to every other party and the Arbitrator in writing any relationships of a nature described in paragraph B.1. not previously identified and disclosed by the Arbitrator.

3. The parties and the Arbitrator are satisfied that any relationships disclosed pursuant to paragraphs B.1. and B.2. will not affect the Arbitrator's independence or impartiality. Notwithstanding such relationships or others the Arbitrator and the parties did not discover

despite good faith efforts, the parties wish the Arbitrator to serve in the Proceeding, waiving any claim based on said relationships, and the Arbitrator agrees to so serve.

4. The disclosure obligations in paragraphs B.1. and B.2. are continuing until the Proceeding is concluded. The ability of the Arbitrator to continue serving in this capacity shall be explored with each such disclosure.

C. Future Relationships

[NOTE: The circumstances under which the arbitrator or the arbitrator's law firm, exclusive of the arbitrator, should be permitted to represent a party to the arbitration in the future on matters unrelated to the arbitration is a subject of debate and does not appear suitable for inclusion in a form of model agreement. However, the parties and the arbitrator may be well advised to include a section dealing with this subject in their agreement.]

D. Compensation

1. The Arbitrator shall be compensated for all time expended in connection with the Proceeding at the rate of $_____$, (per hour, per day, flat fee), plus reasonable travel and other out-of-pocket expenses. The Arbitrator's fee shall be shared equally by the parties, subject to Rule 16.3 of the Procedure.

2. The Arbitrator may utilize members and employees of the firm to assist in connection with the Proceeding and may bill the parties for the time expended by any such persons, to the extent and at a rate agreed upon in advance by the parties.

E. Confidentiality

1. The Arbitrator and each of the parties agree to be bound by and to comply faithfully with Rule 17 of the Procedure relating to confidentiality.

2. The Arbitrator shall be disqualified a witness, consultant or expert in any pending or future action relating to the subject matter of the arbitration, including actions between persons not parties to the arbitration.

3. Whenever a party or the Arbitrator, or their agents, employees, experts or attorneys, is requested, pursuant to a subpoena, a request for production of documents or things or other legal process, to disclose to persons or entities not party to this arbitration, any information regarding the process, including any transcripts, documents, things or testimony, prior to responding thereto such party or Arbitrators shall immediately notify the other party, or in the case of the Arbitrator, both parties, of the existence and terms of such request.

[4. Within [x] days after termination of the arbitration, each party and the Arbitrator shall, at the election of the party furnishing the same, destroy or return all documents, transcripts or other things, and any copies thereof, as well as all summaries or other materials containing or disclosing information contained in, or directly related to, such documents, transcripts or things. Each party and the Arbitrator shall so certify under oath.]

[5. The parties and the Arbitrator agree that damages are not adequate, and no adequate remedy at law exists for any threatened or actual disclosure or use of information in violation of this Section E of this Agreement. Accordingly, each consents to the entry of an injunction against threatened or actual disclosure or use of the information in violation of this Section E of this Agreement.]

F. Immunity

The Arbitrator shall not be liable to any party for any act or omission in connection with any arbitration conducted under the Procedure.

_____   _____
　　　Party　　　　　　　　　　　　　　　　Party

by _____   by _____
　　Party's Attorney　　　　　　　　　　Party's Attorney

_____
　　　Arbitrator

239

APPENDIX G

ABBREVIATED CLAUSES FOR STANDARD BUSINESS AGREEMENTS

© 2002 **CPR Institute for Dispute Resolution**, 366 Madison Avenue, New York, NY 10017-3122; (212) 949-6490, www.cpradr.org. This **excerpt** from **CPR Abbreviated Clauses for Standard Business Agreements** reprinted with permission of **CPR Institute**.

The **CPR Institute** is a nonprofit initiative of 500 general counsel of major corporations, leading law firms and prominent legal academics whose mission is to install alternative dispute resolution (ADR) into the mainstream of legal practice.

Abbreviated Clauses. The following short-form clauses that reflect the recommended multi-step ADR scheme can be used in standard business agreements or in spot transactions such as purchase order forms. Mediation, with arbitration if necessary, is a multi-step process.

Optional clauses to protect rights during ADR appear below.

Negotiation Clause

The parties shall attempt in good faith to resolve any dispute arising out of or relating to this Agreement promptly by negotiation between executives.

Mediation Clause

The parties shall endeavor to resolve any dispute arising out of or relating to this Agreement by mediation under the CPR Mediation Procedure. Unless otherwise agreed, the parties will select a mediator from the CPR Panels of Distinguished Neutrals.

Mediation, With Arbitration if Necessary

The Parties shall endeavor to resolve any dispute arising out of or relating to this agreement by mediation under the CPR Mediation Procedure. Unless the parties agree otherwise, the mediator will be selected from the CPR Panels of Distinguished Neutrals. Any controversy or claim arising out of or relating to this contract or the breach, termination or validity thereof, which remains unresolved 45 days after appointment of a mediator, shall be settled by arbitration by [a sole] [three] arbitrator(s) in accordance with the CPR Rules for Non-Administered Arbitration, and judgment upon the award rendered by the arbitrator(s) may be entered by any court having jurisdiction thereof.

Arbitration Clause

Any dispute arising out of or relating to this contract, including breach, termination or validity thereof, shall be settled by arbitration by [a sole] [three] arbitrator(s) in accordance with the CPR Rules for Non-Administered Arbitration, and judgment upon the award rendered by the arbitrator(s) may be entered by any court having jurisdiction thereof.

Detailed ADR Clauses for Business Agreements

© 2002 **CPR Institute for Dispute Resolution**, 366 Madison Avenue, New York, NY 10017-3122; (212) 949-6490, www.cpradr.org. This **excerpt** from **CPR Detailed ADR Clauses for Business Agreements** reprinted with permission of **CPR Institute**.

The **CPR Institute** is a nonprofit initiative of 500 general counsel of major corporations, leading law firms and prominent legal academics whose mission is to install alternative dispute resolution (ADR) into the mainstream of legal practice.

This section offers detailed multi-step clauses reflecting a variety of drafting options for more detailed agreements. If no binding resolution clause is included, litigation, by default, would remain the means of dispute resolution.

Preamble

Any dispute arising out of or relating to this Agreement shall be resolved in accordance with the procedures specified in this Article, which shall be the sole and exclusive procedures for the resolution of any such disputes.

Negotiation Clauses

Negotiation Between Executives

The parties shall attempt in good faith to resolve any dispute arising out of or relating to this Agreement promptly by negotiation between executives who have authority to settle the controversy and who are at a higher level of management than the persons with direct responsibility for administration of this contract. Any party may give the other party written notice of any dispute not resolved in the normal course of business. Within [15] days after delivery of the notice, the receiving party shall submit to the other a written response. The notice and the response shall include (a) a statement of each party's position and a summary of arguments supporting that position, and (b) the name and title of the executive who will represent that party and of any other person who will accompany the executive. Within [30] days after delivery of the disputing party's notice, the executives of both parties shall meet at a mutually acceptable time and place, and thereafter as often as they reasonably deem necessary, to attempt to resolve this dispute. All reasonable requests for information made by one party to the other will be honored.

All negotiations pursuant to this clause are confidential and shall be treated as compromise and settlement negotiations for purposes of applicable rules of evidence.

Commentary

Negotiation is, of course, the time-honored initial step in attempting to resolve disputes. However, because it can be difficult for the representatives of the parties who are directly involved in a dispute to resolve it, this clause requires, in the event of impasse between the initial negotiators, that the dispute be referred to senior executives of the parties whose presumably greater objectivity may make a successful resolution more likely.

Step Negotiations (Option)

If the matter has not been resolved by these persons within [45] days of the disputing party's notice, the dispute shall be referred to more senior executives of both parties who have authority to settle the dispute and who shall likewise meet to attempt to resolve the dispute.

Commentary

A variant of the ongoing negotiation procedure is the "step negotiation" technique under which the intermediate executives to whom the dispute has been referred will be required, if they are unsuccessful in resolving the problem, to refer the problem to more senior executives. A step negotiation clause would add the above provision to the "Negotiation Between Executives" clause, above.

Mediation Clauses

Mediation

If the dispute has not been resolved by negotiation within [45] days of the disputing party's notice, or if the parties failed to meet within [20] days, the parties shall endeavor to settle the dispute by mediation under the [then current] CPR Mediation Procedure [in effect on the date of this agreement]. Unless otherwise agreed, the parties will select a mediator from the CPR Panels of Distinguished Neutrals.

Mediation With Designated Neutral (Option)

If the dispute has not been resolved by negotiation within [45] days of the disputing party's notice, or if the parties failed to meet within [20] days, the parties shall endeavor to settle the dispute by mediation under the [then current] CPR Mediation Procedure [in effect on the date of this agreement]. The parties have selected _____ as the mediator in any such dispute, and [he] [she] has agreed to serve in that capacity and to be available on reasonable notice. In the event that _____ becomes unwilling or unable to serve, the parties have selected _____ as the alternative mediator. In the event that neither _____ nor _____ is willing or able to serve, the parties will agree on a substitute with the assistance of CPR. Unless otherwise agreed, the parties will select a mediator from the CPR Panels of Distinguished Neutrals.

Commentary

It is often easier to agree on a neutral (or on the process for selecting a neutral) before any dispute actually arises. The neutral can be available for swift assistance if his or her selection and terms of retention have already been established.

Arbitration Clause

Any dispute arising out of or relating to this contract including the breach, termination or validity thereof [which has not been resolved by a non-binding procedure as provided herein within [90] days of the initiation of such procedure,] shall be settled by arbitration in accordance with the CPR Rules for Non-Administered Arbitration [in effect on the date of this agreement,] by [a sole arbitrator] [three independent and impartial arbitrators, of whom each party shall appoint one], [three arbitrators, of whom the party shall designate one in accordance with the "screened" appointment procedure provided in Rule 5.4] [three arbitrators, none of whom shall be appointed by either party]; [provided, however, that if either party will not participate in a non-binding procedure; the other may initiate arbitration before expiration of the above period.] The arbitration shall be governed by the Federal Arbitration Act, 9 U.S.C. §§ 1–16, and judgment upon the award rendered by the arbitrator(s) may be entered by any court having jurisdiction thereof. The place of arbitration shall be _____. [The arbitrator(s) are not empowered to award damages in excess of compensatory damages [and each party expressly waives and foregoes any right to punitive, exemplary or similar damages unless a statute requires that compensatory damages be increased in a specified manner.]]

The statute of limitations of the State of _____ applicable to the commencement of a lawsuit shall apply to the commencement of an arbitration hereunder, except that no defenses shall be available based upon the passage of time during any negotiation or mediation called for by the preceding paragraphs of this Article.

-or-

Litigation Clause

If the dispute has not been resolved by non-binding means as provided herein within 90 days of the initiation of such procedure, either party may initiate litigation [upon ___ days written notice to the other party]; provided, however, that if one party has requested the other to participate in a non-binding procedure and the other has failed to participate, the requesting party may initiate litigation before expiration of the above period.

Commentary

If non-binding procedures are unsuccessful and if the parties have not agreed on a binding ADR procedure, presumably they may go to court.

CPR Model Master Dispute Resolution Agreement (Negotiation-Mediation-Litigation)

© 2002 **CPR Institute for Dispute Resolution**, 366 Madison Avenue, New York, NY 10017-3122; (212) 949-6490, www.cpradr.org. This **excerpt** from **CPR Model Master Dispute Resolution Agreement** (Negotiation-Mediation-Litigation) reprinted with permission of **CPR Institute**.

The **CPR Institute** is a nonprofit initiative of 500 general counsel of major corporations, leading law firms and prominent legal academics whose mission is to install alternative dispute resolution (ADR) into the mainstream of legal practice.

AGREEMENT dated _____ between X Corporation and Y Corporation.

X Corporation and Y Corporation have entered into business arrangements in the past and may well enter into further agreements hereafter. These agreements have taken the form of purchase orders, sales orders, negotiated contracts, or _____ ("Business Agreements"). Such agreements may lead to disputes that are not resolved by the regularly responsible persons in the normal course of business.

Both companies agree that efforts shall be made to resolve any future dispute arising out of or relating to any past or future agreement between them (the "Dispute") in an amicable manner, in accordance with the procedures specified hereinbelow.

1. Negotiation

When a Dispute has arisen and negotiations between the regularly responsible persons have reached an impasse, either party may give the other party written notice of the Dispute. In the event such notice is given, the parties shall attempt to resolve the Dispute promptly by negotiation between executives who have authority to settle the controversy and who are at a higher level of management than the persons with direct responsibility for the matter. Within [10] days after delivery of the notice, the receiving party shall submit to the other a written response. Thereafter, the executives shall confer in person or by telephone promptly to attempt to resolve the dispute. All reasonable requests for information made by one party to the other will be honored.

2. Mediation

If the dispute has not been resolved by negotiation within [30] days of the disputing party's notice, or if the parties have failed to confer within [20] days after delivery of the notice, the parties shall endeavor to settle the dispute by mediation under the CPR Mediation Procedure in effect on the date of this Agreement. Unless otherwise agreed, the parties will select a mediator from the CPR Panels of Distinguished Neutrals.

All negotiations and proceedings pursuant to paragraphs 1. and 2. are confidential and shall be treated as compromise and settlement negotiations for purposes of applicable rules of evidence and any additional confidentiality protections provided by applicable law.

3. Litigation

If the dispute has not been resolved by mediation as provided herein within 90 days of the initiation of such procedure, either party may initiate litigation, unless the agreement under which the Dispute arose provides for arbitration; provided that if one party has requested the other to participate in a mediation procedure and the other has failed to participate, and their agreement does not provide for arbitration, the requesting party may initiate litigation before expiration of the above period.

Optional language:

Moreover, a party may file a complaint at any time to establish venue (if the parties' agreement does not provide for arbitration), or to seek a preliminary injunction or other provisional judicial relief, if in its sole judgment such action is necessary. Despite such action the parties will continue to participate in the procedures specified in this Agreement.

The parties agree that if they engage in litigation, both irrevocably waive (a) exemplary, punitive or any other damages in excess of compensatory damages; and (b) trial by jury.

4. Tolling Statute of Limitations

All applicable statutes of limitation and defenses based upon the passage of time shall be tolled while the procedures specified in paragraphs 1. and 2. of this Agreement are pending. The parties will take such action, if any, required to effectuate such tolling.

5. Termination of Business Agreement

This Agreement shall not be deemed a waiver of any right of termination under the Business Agreement out of which the Dispute arose. Unless either party has such a right and has exercised the same, each party shall continue to perform its obligations under such agreement pending resolution of the Dispute.

6. Governing Law

The law governing the Business Agreement shall govern this Agreement.

7. Governing Agreement

In the event of a conflict between the provisions of this Agreement and the dispute resolution provisions specified in any Business Agreement entered into before [or after] this Agreement, the provisions of this Agreement shall govern. A clause calling for binding arbitration shall not be deemed in conflict with this Agreement, but the procedures hereunder shall be followed to conclusion before the arbitration clause is invoked.

8. Termination of Agreement

This Agreement may be terminated by either party on written notice to the other party as to Business Agreements entered into after such notice is given. Such termination shall not affect any Dispute under any Business Agreement between the parties entered into at any time before such notice was given.

X Corporation

by _____

Y Corporation

by _____

[Note: This form as drafted covers all disputes between the parties. The form may be modified either to limit its coverage to specified types of disputes, or to carve out certain types of disputes. The form also may be modified to cover only disputes arising out of future agreements between the parties.

If this form of agreement is adopted, it may be advisable to include a sentence in future business agreements to the effect that the master dispute resolution agreement between the parties shall apply as to any disputes arising under the business agreement.]

CPR Model Master Dispute Resolution Agreement (Negotiation-Mediation-Arbitration mdrF.1)

© 2002 **CPR Institute for Dispute Resolution**, 366 Madison Avenue, New York, NY 10017-3122; (212) 949-6490, www.cpradr.org. This **excerpt** from **CPR Model Master Dispute Resolution Agreement** (Negotiation-Mediation-Arbitration Master **mdrF.1**) reprinted with permission of **CPR Institute.**

The **CPR Institute** is a nonprofit initiative of 500 general counsel of major corporations, leading law firms and prominent legal academics whose mission is to install alternative dispute resolution (ADR) into the mainstream of legal practice.

AGREEMENT dated _____ between X Corporation and Y Corporation.

X Corporation and Y Corporation have entered into business agreements in the past and may well enter into further agreements hereafter. These agreements have taken the form of purchase orders, sales orders, negotiated contracts, or _____("Business Agreements") Such agreements may lead to disputes that are not resolved by the regularly responsible persons in the normal course of business.

Both companies agree to resolve any future dispute arising out of or relating to any past or future agreement between them (the "Dispute") in accordance with the procedures specified hereinbelow.

1. Negotiation

When a Dispute has arisen and negotiations between the regularly responsible persons have reached an impasse, either party may give the other party written notice of the Dispute. In the event such notice is given, the parties shall attempt to resolve the Dispute promptly by negotiation between executives who have authority to settle the controversy and who are at a higher level of management than the persons with direct responsibility for the matter. Within [10] days after delivery of the notice, the receiving party shall submit to the other a written response. Thereafter, the executives shall confer in person or by telephone promptly to attempt to resolve the dispute. All reasonable requests for information made by one party to the other will be honored.

2. Mediation

If the dispute has not been resolved by negotiation within [30] days of the disputing party's notice, or if the parties have failed to confer within [20] days after delivery of the notice, the parties shall endeavor to settle the dispute by mediation under the CPR Mediation Procedure in effect on the date of this Agreement. Unless otherwise agreed, the parties will select a mediator from the CPR Panels of Distinguished Neutrals.

All negotiations and proceedings pursuant to paragraphs 1. and 2. are confidential and shall be treated as compromise and settlement negotiations for purposes of applicable rules of evidence and any additional confidentiality protections provided by applicable law.

3. Arbitration

If the dispute has not been resolved by mediation as provided herein within [90] days of the initiation of such procedure, it shall be settled by binding arbitration in accordance with the CPR Rules for Non-Administered Arbitration in effect on the date of this agreement, by a sole arbitrator selected from the CPR Panel, except that if the amount in controversy exceeds $_____, either party may opt for an arbitration conducted by three independent and impartial arbitrators, none of whom shall be appointed by either party; provided, however, that if either party will not participate in a mediation, the other may initiate arbitration before expiration of the above period. The arbitration shall be governed by the Federal Arbitration Act, 9 U.S.C.§ 1–16 to the exclusion of state laws inconsistent therewith, and judgment upon the award rendered by the arbitrator(s) may be entered by any court having jurisdiction thereof. The place of arbitration shall be _____.

[The arbitrator(s) are not empowered to award damages in excess of compensatory damages, and each party hereby irrevocably waives any right to recover such damages with respect to any dispute between them resolved by arbitration.]

The statute of limitations of the State of _____ applicable to the commencement of a lawsuit shall apply to the commencement of an arbitration hereunder, except that no defenses shall be available based upon the passage of time during any negotiation or mediation called for by the preceding sections of this Agreement.

4. Provisional Judicial Relief (Optional)

A party may file a complaint at any time before an arbitrator(s) (has) (have) been selected to seek a preliminary injunction or other provisional judicial relief, if in its sole judgment such action is necessary. Despite such action the parties will continue to participate in the procedures specified in this Agreement.

5. Termination of Business Agreement

This Agreement shall not be deemed a waiver of any right of termination under the Business Agreement out of which the Dispute arose. Unless either party has such a right and has exercised the same, each party shall continue to perform its obligations under such agreement pending resolution of the Dispute.

6. Governing Law

The law governing the Business Agreement shall govern this Agreement.

7. Governing Agreement

In the event of a conflict between the provisions of this Agreement and the dispute resolution provisions specified in any Business Agreement entered into before [or after] this Agreement, the provisions of this Agreement shall govern.

8. Termination of Agreement

This Agreement may be terminated by either party on written notice to the other party as to Business Agreements entered into after such notice is given. Such termination shall not affect any Dispute under any Business Agreement between the parties entered into at any time before such notice was given.

X Corporation

by_____

Y Corporation

by_____

[Note: This form as drafted covers all disputes between the parties. The form may be modified to limit the negotiation, mediation or arbitration coverage to specified types of disputes, or to carve out certain types of disputes. The form also may be modified to cover only disputes arising out of future agreements between the parties.

If this form of agreement is adopted, it may be advisable to include a sentence in future business agreements to the effect that the master dispute resolution agreement between the parties shall apply as to any disputes arising under the business agreement.]

BIBLIOGRAPHY

American Arbitration Association. "Mediator Training Manual." Atlanta, Georgia, 1992.

Bolton, R. *People Skills.* New York: Simon & Schuster, 1979.

Center for Public Resources, Inc. "Model ADR Procedures—Mediation of Business Disputes." New York, 1991.

Cooley, J. "Arbitration vs. Mediation—Explaining the Differences." *Judicature* vol. 69, no. 5, 18–24 (Feb.–March 1986).

CDR Associates. "Decision Making and Conflict Management: An Overview." Boulder, Colorado, 1991.

CDR Associates. "Mediation." Boulder, Colorado, 1991.

CDR Associates. "Negotiation." Boulder, Colorado, 1991.

Fisher, R. and W. Ury. *Getting to Yes—Negotiating Agreement Without Giving In.* New York: Penguin Books, 1983.

"Important Issues in Arbitration Law Recently Decided or on the Horizon," R. Dokson, Alternative Dispute Resolution Institute Program Materials (Ga. 2001).

Karrass, C., *The Negotiating Game.* New York: Harper Collins, 1992.

Leeson, S. and B. Johnston. *Ending It: Dispute Resolution in America—Descriptions, Examples, Cases and Questions.* Cincinnati, Ohio: Anderson, 1988.

Moore, C. *The Mediation Process—Practical Strategies for Resolving Conflict.* San Francisco: Jossey-Bass, 1991.

Riskin, L. and J. Westbrook. *Dispute Resolution and Lawyers.* Abridged edition. St. Paul, Minnesota: West, 1987.

Ury, W., J. Brett, and S. Goldberg. *Getting Disputes Resolved.* San Francisco: Jossey-Bass, 1989.

Ury, W. *Getting Past No—Negotiating with Difficult People.* New York: Bantam, 1991.

Ury, W. *The Third Side.* New York: Penguin Books, 2000.

Williams, G. *Legal Negotiation and Settlement.* St. Paul, Minnesota: West, 1983.